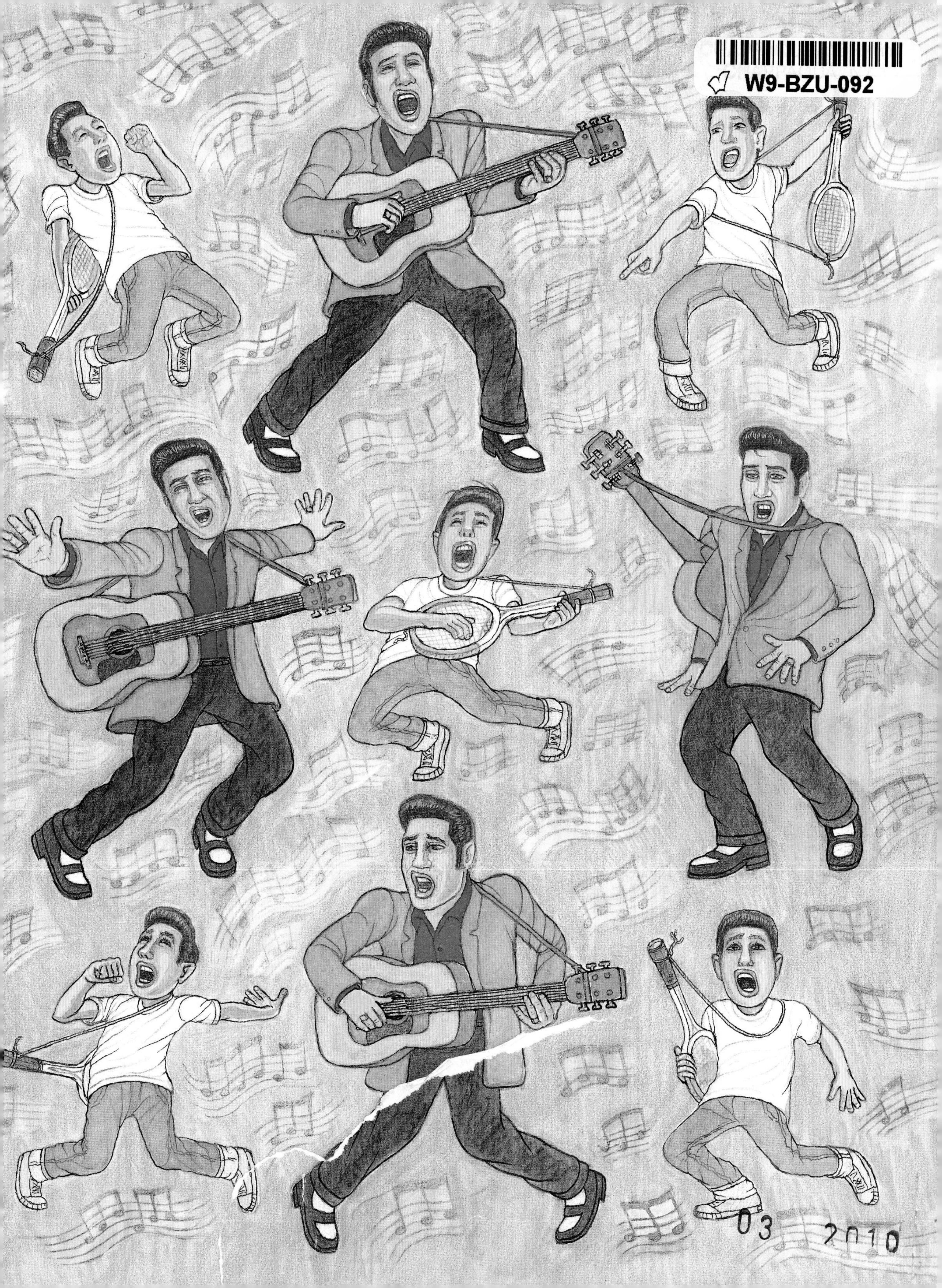

SHAKE, RATTLE & TURN THAT NOISE DOWN!

HOW ELVIS SHOOK UP MUSIC, ME AND MOM

MARK ALAN STAMATY

NOTHIN' BUT A WHAT?!

Alfred A. Knopf
NEW YORK

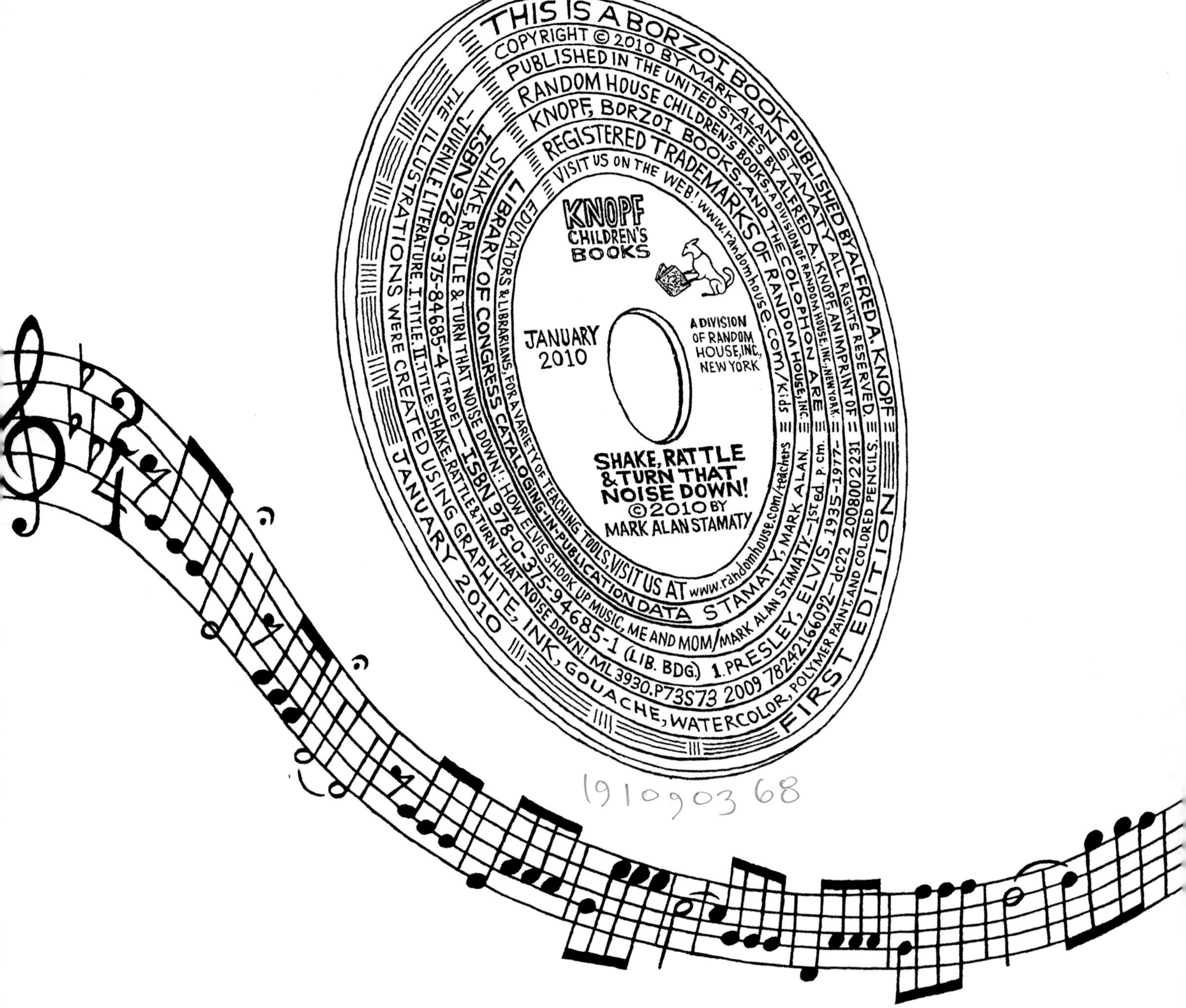
THIS IS A BORZOI BOOK PUBLISHED BY ALFRED A. KNOPF
COPYRIGHT © 2010 BY MARK ALAN STAMATY ALL RIGHTS RESERVED.
PUBLISHED IN THE UNITED STATES BY ALFRED A. KNOPF, AN IMPRINT OF RANDOM HOUSE CHILDREN'S BOOKS, A DIVISION OF RANDOM HOUSE, INC., NEW YORK.
KNOPF, BORZOI BOOKS, AND THE COLOPHON ARE REGISTERED TRADEMARKS OF RANDOM HOUSE, INC.
VISIT US ON THE WEB! www.randomhouse.com/kids
EDUCATORS & LIBRARIANS, FOR A VARIETY OF TEACHING TOOLS, VISIT US AT www.randomhouse.com/teachers
LIBRARY OF CONGRESS CATALOGING-IN-PUBLICATION DATA
STAMATY, MARK ALAN.
SHAKE, RATTLE & TURN THAT NOISE DOWN! : HOW ELVIS SHOOK UP MUSIC, ME AND MOM / MARK ALAN STAMATY.—1st ed. p. cm.
ISBN 978-0-375-84685-4 (TRADE) — ISBN 978-0-375-94685-1 (LIB. BDG.)
1. PRESLEY, ELVIS, 1935–1977—JUVENILE LITERATURE. I. TITLE. II. TITLE: SHAKE, RATTLE & TURN THAT NOISE DOWN!
ML3930.P73S73 2009 782.42166092—dc22 2008002231
THE ILLUSTRATIONS WERE CREATED USING GRAPHITE, INK, GOUACHE, WATERCOLOR, POLYMER PAINT, AND COLORED PENCILS.
JANUARY 2010
FIRST EDITION
KNOPF CHILDREN'S BOOKS
JANUARY 2010
A DIVISION OF RANDOM HOUSE, INC., NEW YORK
SHAKE, RATTLE & TURN THAT NOISE DOWN! ©2010 BY MARK ALAN STAMATY

MANUFACTURED IN MALAYSIA
January 2010
10 9 8 7 6 5 4 3 2 1

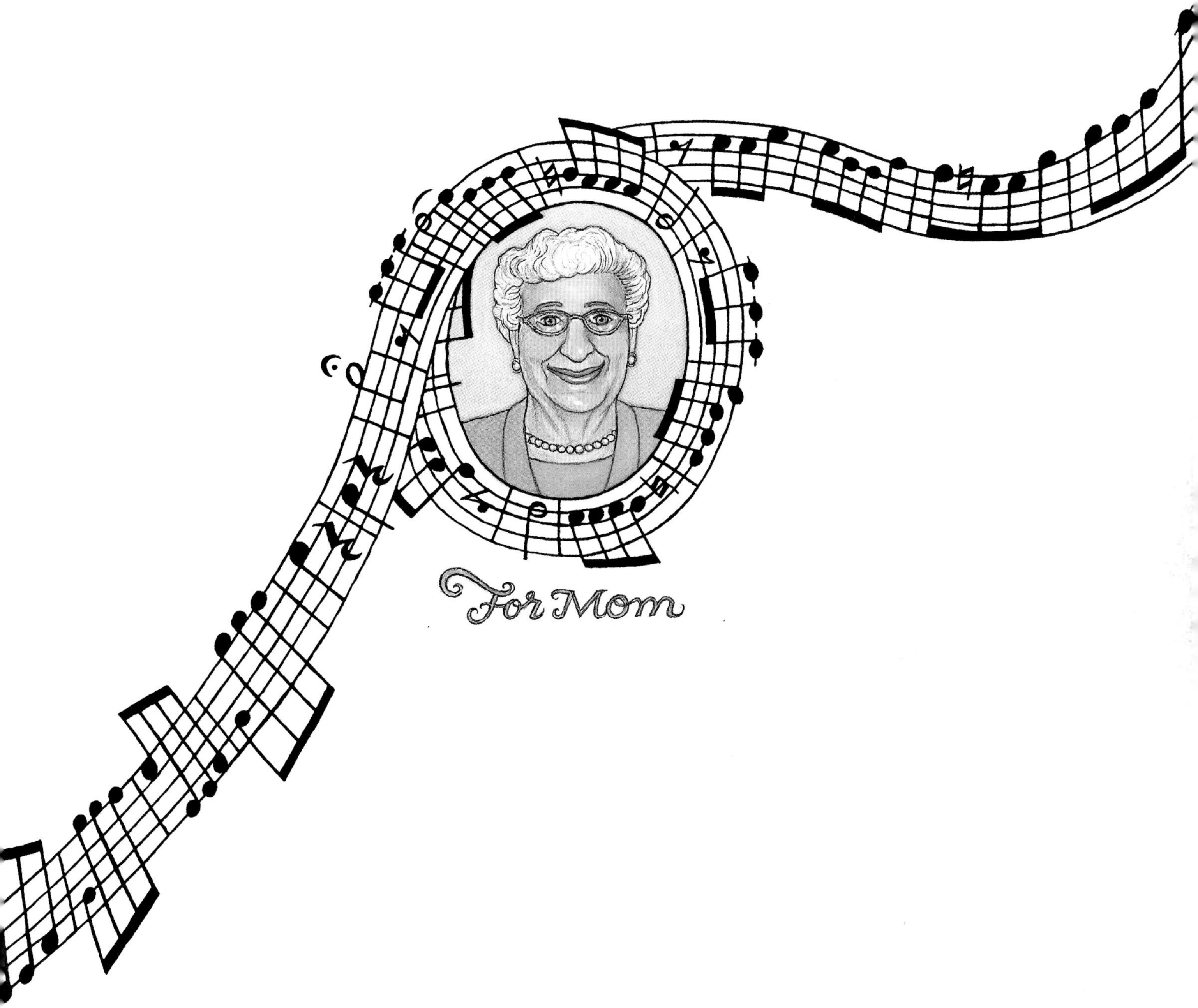

For Mom

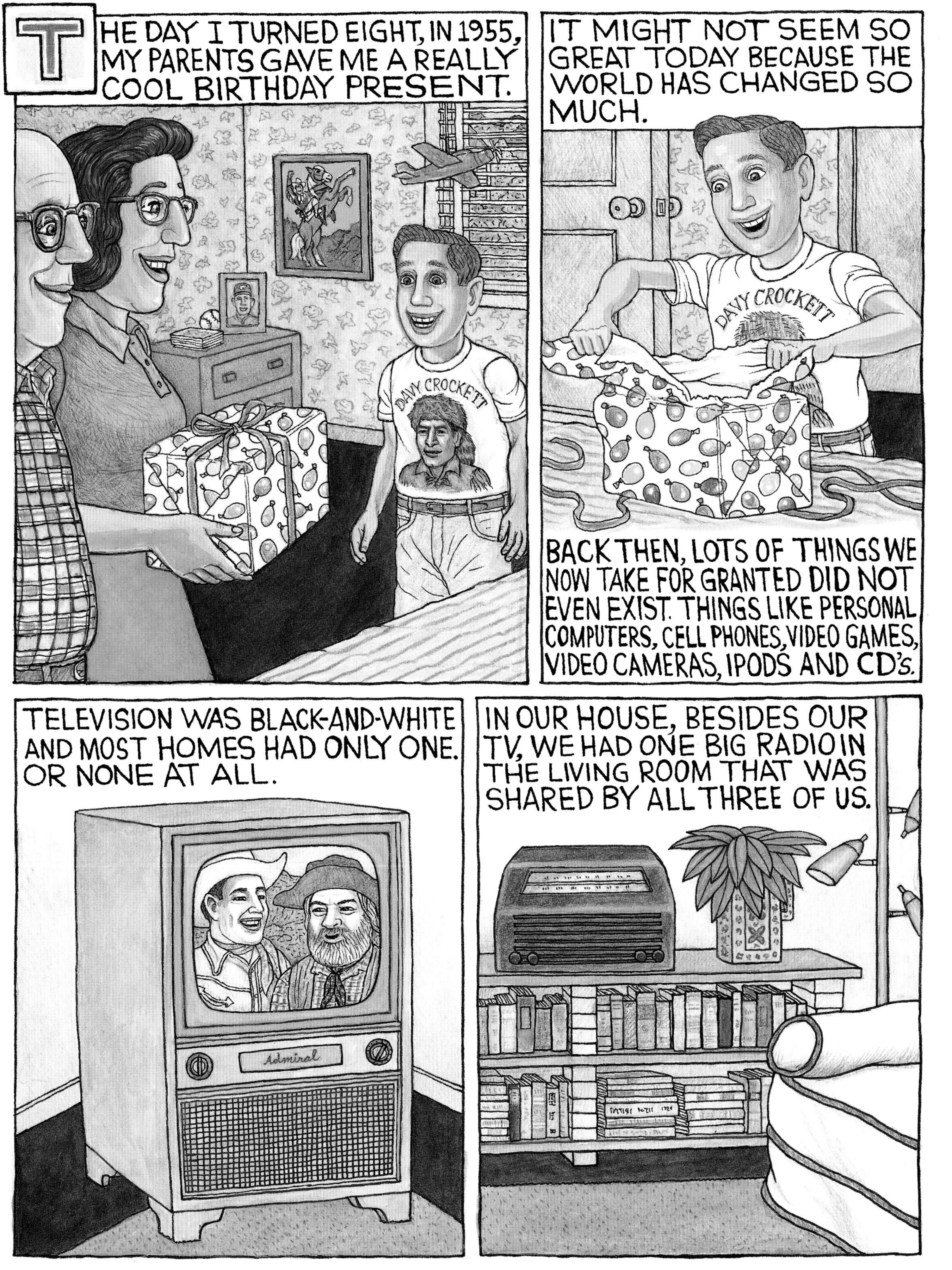
THE DAY I TURNED EIGHT, IN 1955, MY PARENTS GAVE ME A REALLY COOL BIRTHDAY PRESENT.
DAVY CROCKETT
IT MIGHT NOT SEEM SO GREAT TODAY BECAUSE THE WORLD HAS CHANGED SO MUCH.
DAVY CROCKETT
BACK THEN, LOTS OF THINGS WE NOW TAKE FOR GRANTED DID NOT EVEN EXIST. THINGS LIKE PERSONAL COMPUTERS, CELL PHONES, VIDEO GAMES, VIDEO CAMERAS, IPODS AND CD's.
TELEVISION WAS BLACK-AND-WHITE AND MOST HOMES HAD ONLY ONE. OR NONE AT ALL.
Admiral
IN OUR HOUSE, BESIDES OUR TV, WE HAD ONE BIG RADIO IN THE LIVING ROOM THAT WAS SHARED BY ALL THREE OF US.

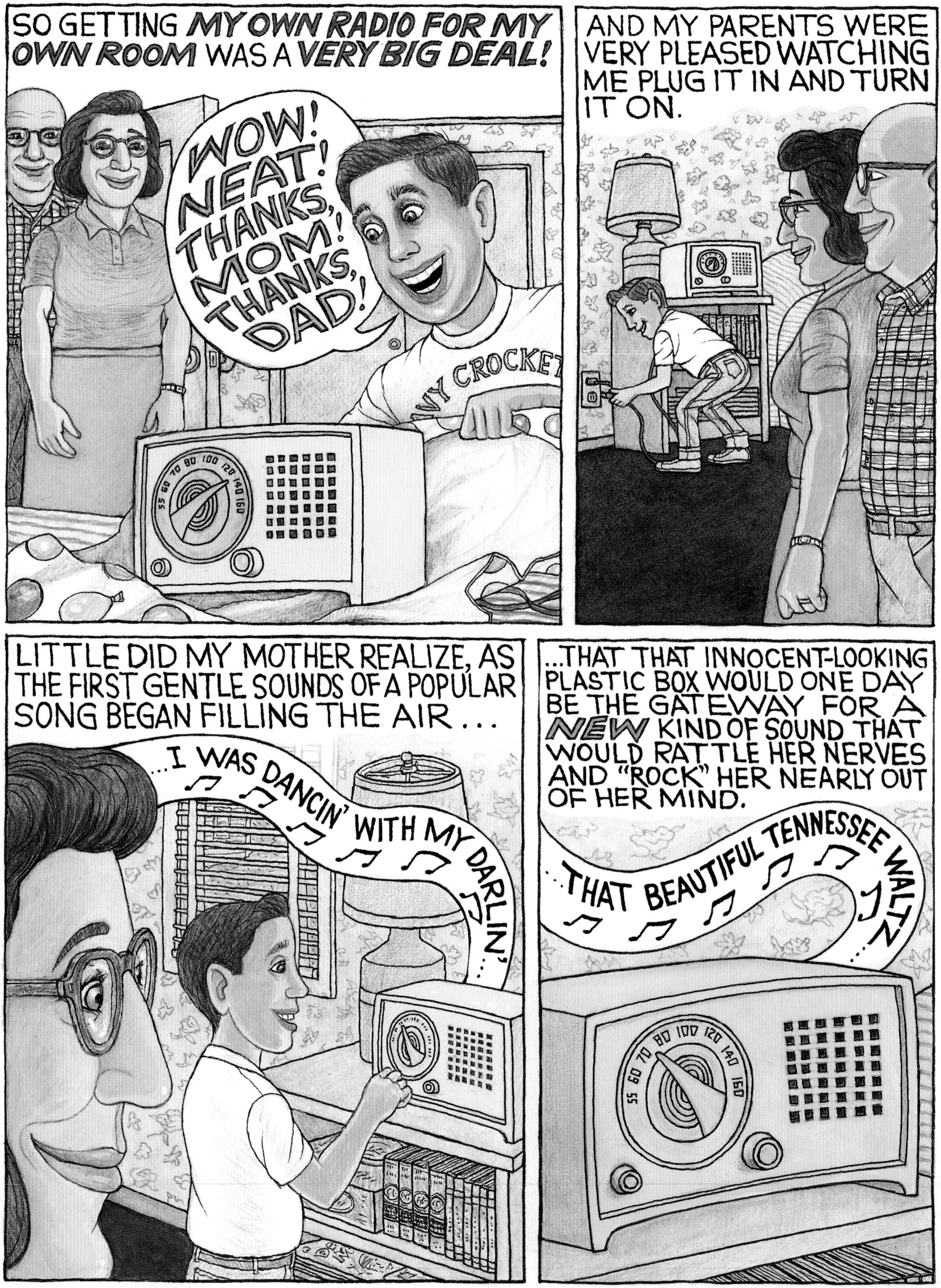
SO GETTING MY OWN RADIO FOR MY OWN ROOM WAS A VERY BIG DEAL!
WOW! NEAT! THANKS, MOM! THANKS, DAD!
VY CROCKET
55 60 70 80 100 120 140 160
AND MY PARENTS WERE VERY PLEASED WATCHING ME PLUG IT IN AND TURN IT ON.
LITTLE DID MY MOTHER REALIZE, AS THE FIRST GENTLE SOUNDS OF A POPULAR SONG BEGAN FILLING THE AIR . . .
...I WAS DANCIN' WITH MY DARLIN'...
...THAT THAT INNOCENT-LOOKING PLASTIC BOX WOULD ONE DAY BE THE GATEWAY FOR A NEW KIND OF SOUND THAT WOULD RATTLE HER NERVES AND "ROCK" HER NEARLY OUT OF HER MIND.
...THAT BEAUTIFUL TENNESSEE WALTZ...
55 60 70 80 100 120 140 160

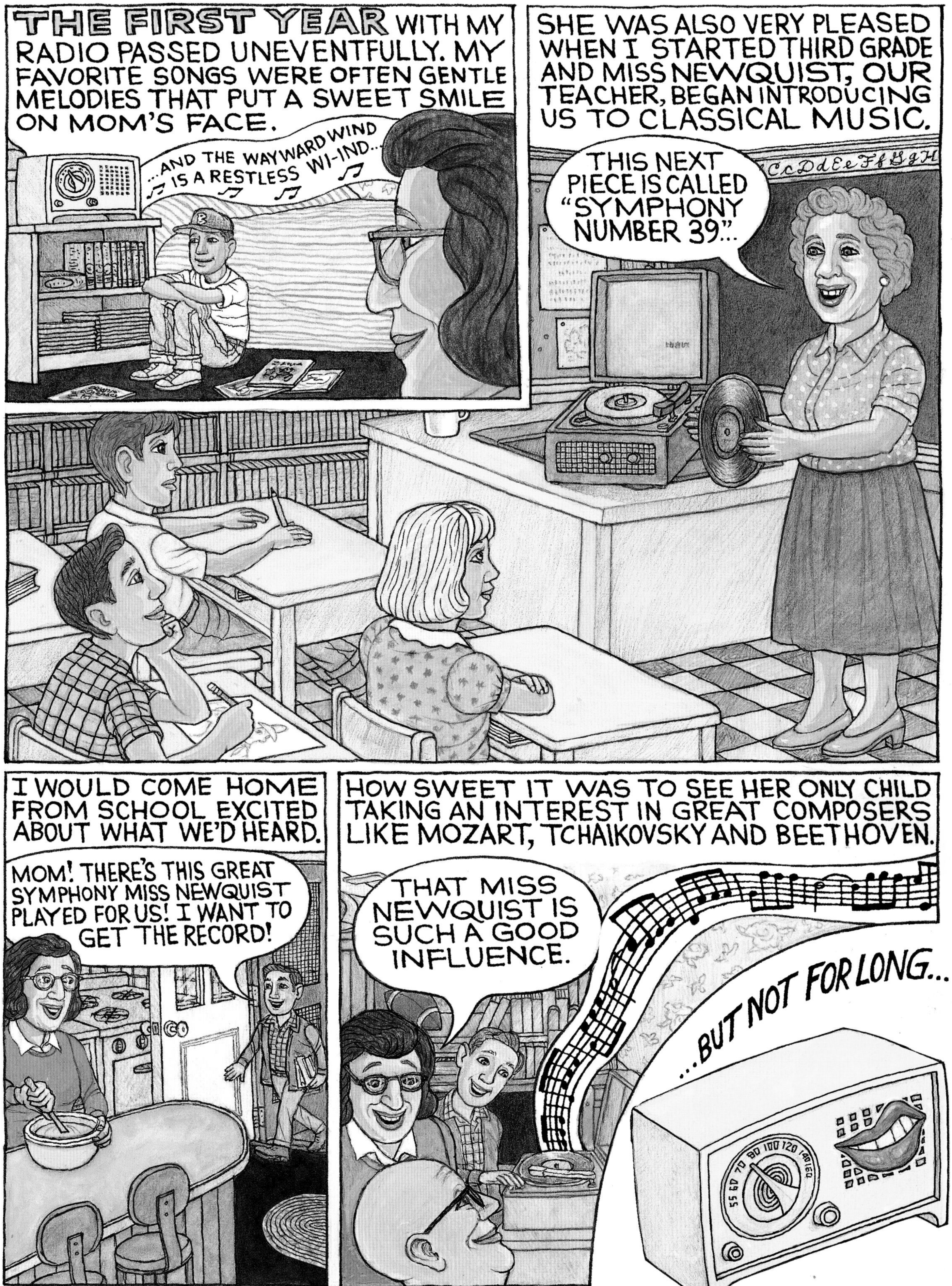
THE FIRST YEAR WITH MY RADIO PASSED UNEVENTFULLY. MY FAVORITE SONGS WERE OFTEN GENTLE MELODIES THAT PUT A SWEET SMILE ON MOM'S FACE.
...AND THE WAYWARD WIND IS A RESTLESS WI-IND...
SHE WAS ALSO VERY PLEASED WHEN I STARTED THIRD GRADE AND MISS NEWQUIST, OUR TEACHER, BEGAN INTRODUCING US TO CLASSICAL MUSIC.
THIS NEXT PIECE IS CALLED "SYMPHONY NUMBER 39."...
I WOULD COME HOME FROM SCHOOL EXCITED ABOUT WHAT WE'D HEARD.
MOM! THERE'S THIS GREAT SYMPHONY MISS NEWQUIST PLAYED FOR US! I WANT TO GET THE RECORD!
HOW SWEET IT WAS TO SEE HER ONLY CHILD TAKING AN INTEREST IN GREAT COMPOSERS LIKE MOZART, TCHAIKOVSKY AND BEETHOVEN.
THAT MISS NEWQUIST IS SUCH A GOOD INFLUENCE.
...BUT NOT FOR LONG...

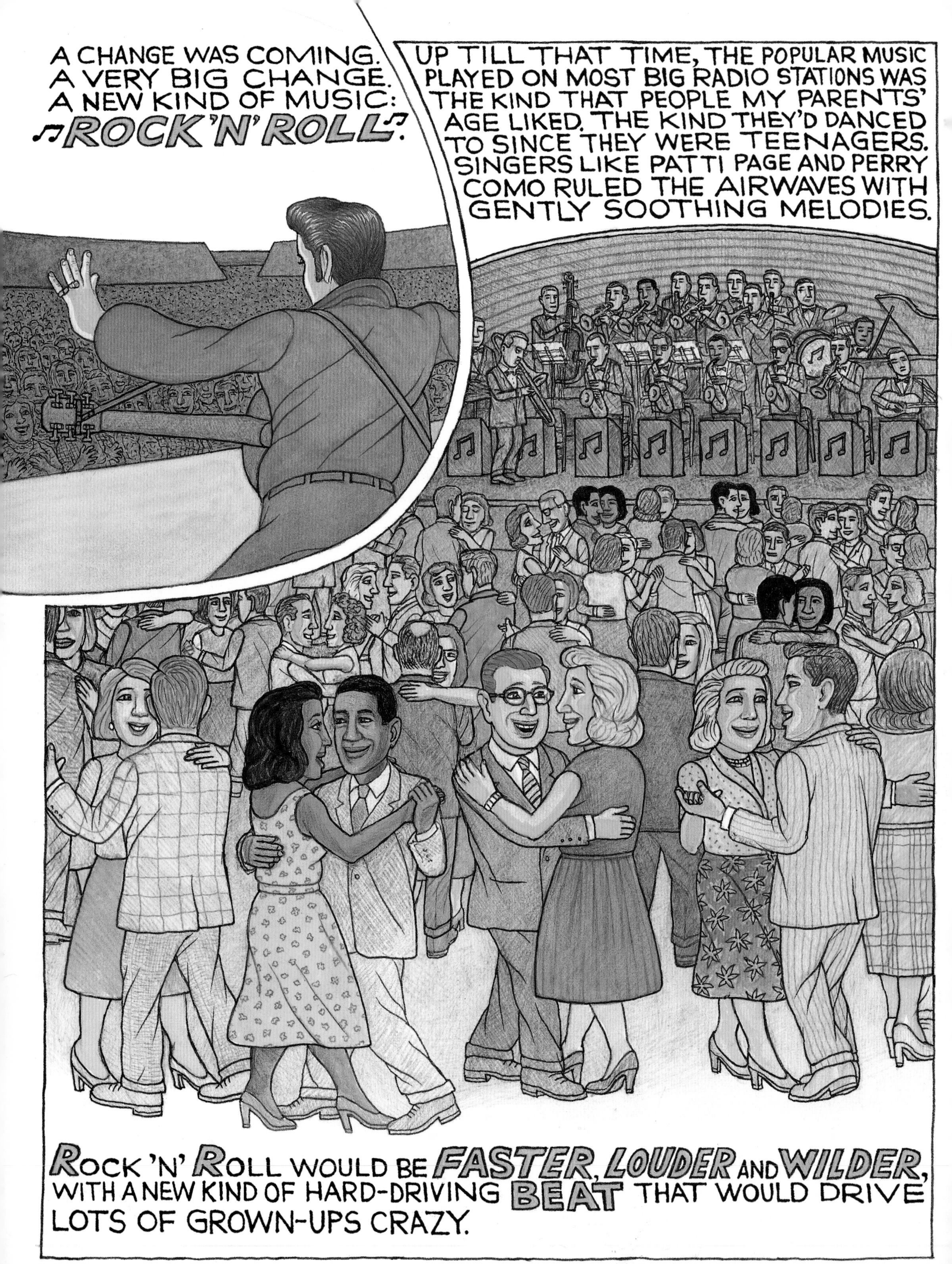
A CHANGE WAS COMING. A VERY BIG CHANGE. A NEW KIND OF MUSIC: ROCK 'N' ROLL.
UP TILL THAT TIME, THE POPULAR MUSIC PLAYED ON MOST BIG RADIO STATIONS WAS THE KIND THAT PEOPLE MY PARENTS' AGE LIKED. THE KIND THEY'D DANCED TO SINCE THEY WERE TEENAGERS. SINGERS LIKE PATTI PAGE AND PERRY COMO RULED THE AIRWAVES WITH GENTLY SOOTHING MELODIES.
ROCK 'N' ROLL WOULD BE FASTER, LOUDER AND WILDER, WITH A NEW KIND OF HARD-DRIVING BEAT THAT WOULD DRIVE LOTS OF GROWN-UPS CRAZY.

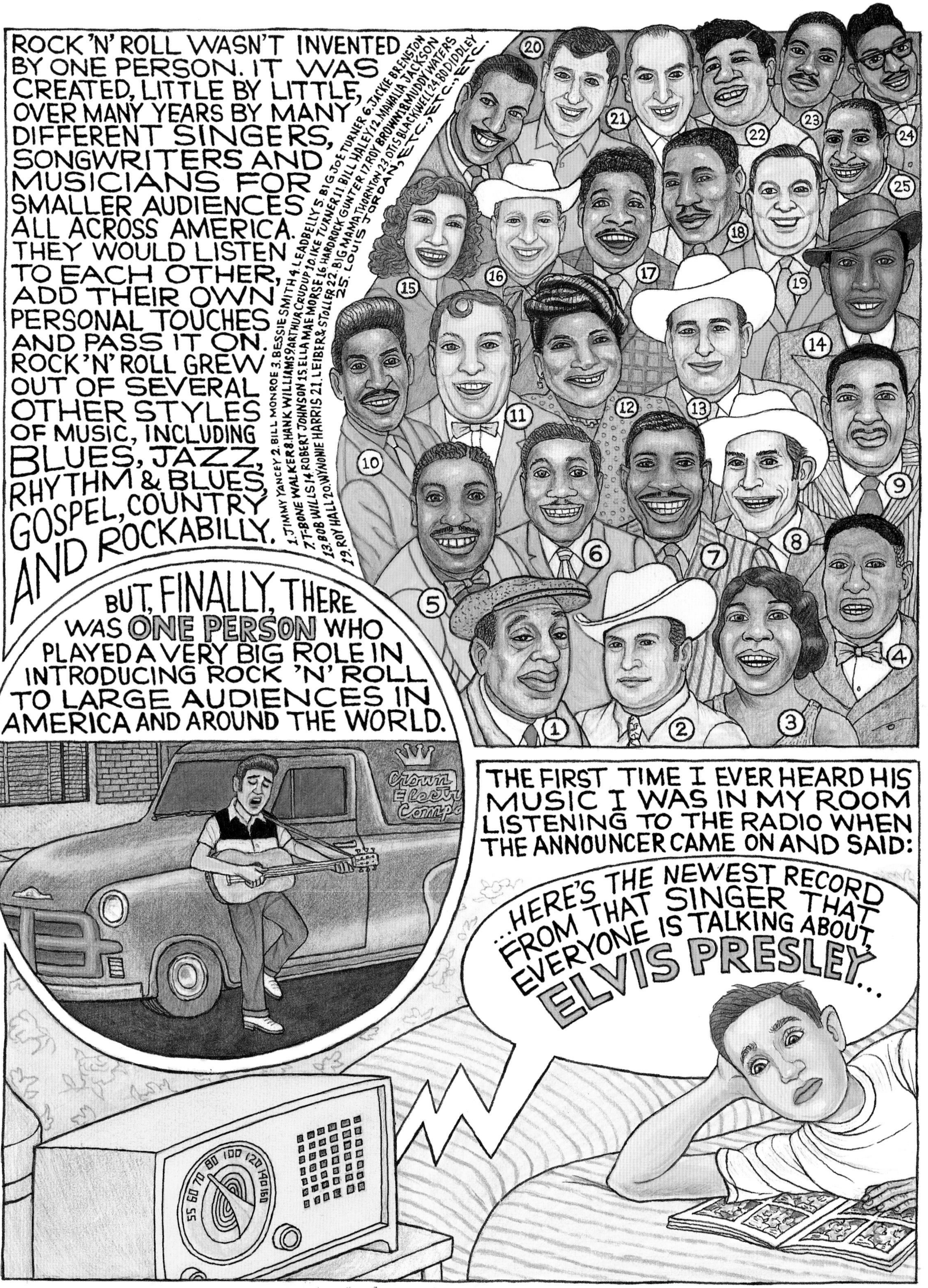
ROCK 'N' ROLL WASN'T INVENTED BY ONE PERSON. IT WAS CREATED, LITTLE BY LITTLE, OVER MANY YEARS BY MANY DIFFERENT SINGERS, SONGWRITERS AND MUSICIANS FOR SMALLER AUDIENCES ALL ACROSS AMERICA. THEY WOULD LISTEN TO EACH OTHER, ADD THEIR OWN PERSONAL TOUCHES AND PASS IT ON. ROCK 'N' ROLL GREW OUT OF SEVERAL OTHER STYLES OF MUSIC, INCLUDING BLUES, JAZZ, RHYTHM & BLUES, GOSPEL, COUNTRY AND ROCKABILLY.
1. JIMMY YANCEY 2. BILL MONROE 3. BESSIE SMITH 4. LEADBELLY 5. BIG JOE TURNER 6. JACKIE BRENSTON
7. T-BONE WALKER 8. HANK WILLIAMS 9. ARTHUR CRUDUP 10. IKE TURNER 11. BILL HALEY 12. MAHALIA JACKSON
13. BOB WILLS 14. ROBERT JOHNSON 15. ELLA MAE MORSE 16. HARDROCK GUNTER 17. ROY BROWN 18. MUDDY WATERS
19. ROY HALL 20. WYNONIE HARRIS 21. LEIBER & STOLLER 22. BIG MAMA THORNTON 23. OTIS BLACKWELL 24. BO DIDDLEY
25. LOUIS JORDAN, ETC., ETC., ETC.
20
21
22
23
24
25
15
16
17
18
19
14
10
11
12
13
9
5
6
7
8
1
2
3
4
BUT, FINALLY, THERE WAS ONE PERSON WHO PLAYED A VERY BIG ROLE IN INTRODUCING ROCK 'N' ROLL TO LARGE AUDIENCES IN AMERICA AND AROUND THE WORLD.
Crown Electric Company
THE FIRST TIME I EVER HEARD HIS MUSIC I WAS IN MY ROOM LISTENING TO THE RADIO WHEN THE ANNOUNCER CAME ON AND SAID:
...HERE'S THE NEWEST RECORD FROM THAT SINGER THAT EVERYONE IS TALKING ABOUT, ELVIS PRESLEY...
55 60 70 80 100 120 140 160

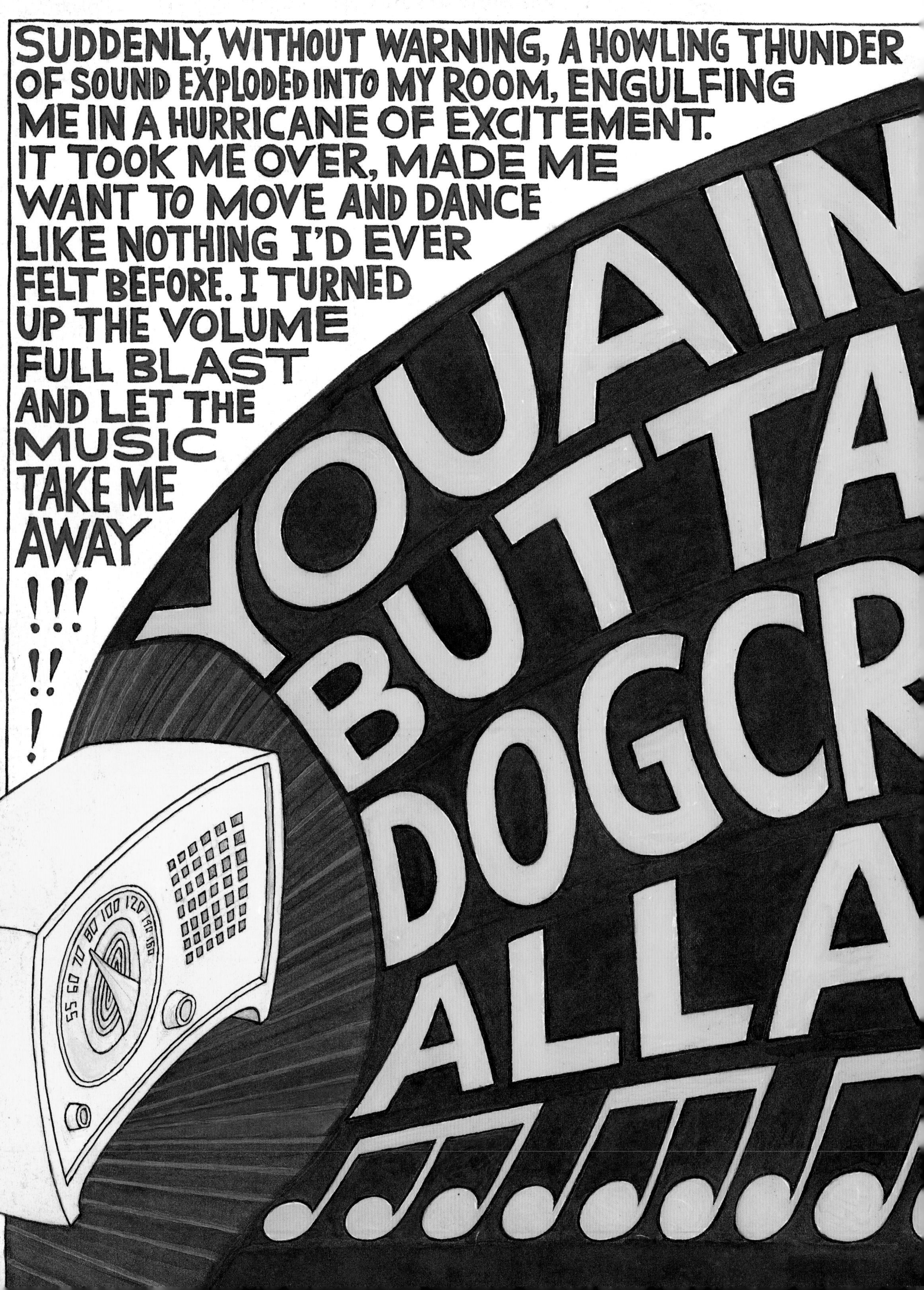
SUDDENLY, WITHOUT WARNING, A HOWLING THUNDER OF SOUND EXPLODED INTO MY ROOM, ENGULFING ME IN A HURRICANE OF EXCITEMENT. IT TOOK ME OVER, MADE ME WANT TO MOVE AND DANCE LIKE NOTHING I'D EVER FELT BEFORE. I TURNED UP THE VOLUME FULL BLAST AND LET THE MUSIC TAKE ME AWAY !!!!!!
YOUAIN
BUTTA
DOGCR
ALLA
55 60 70 80 100 120 140 160

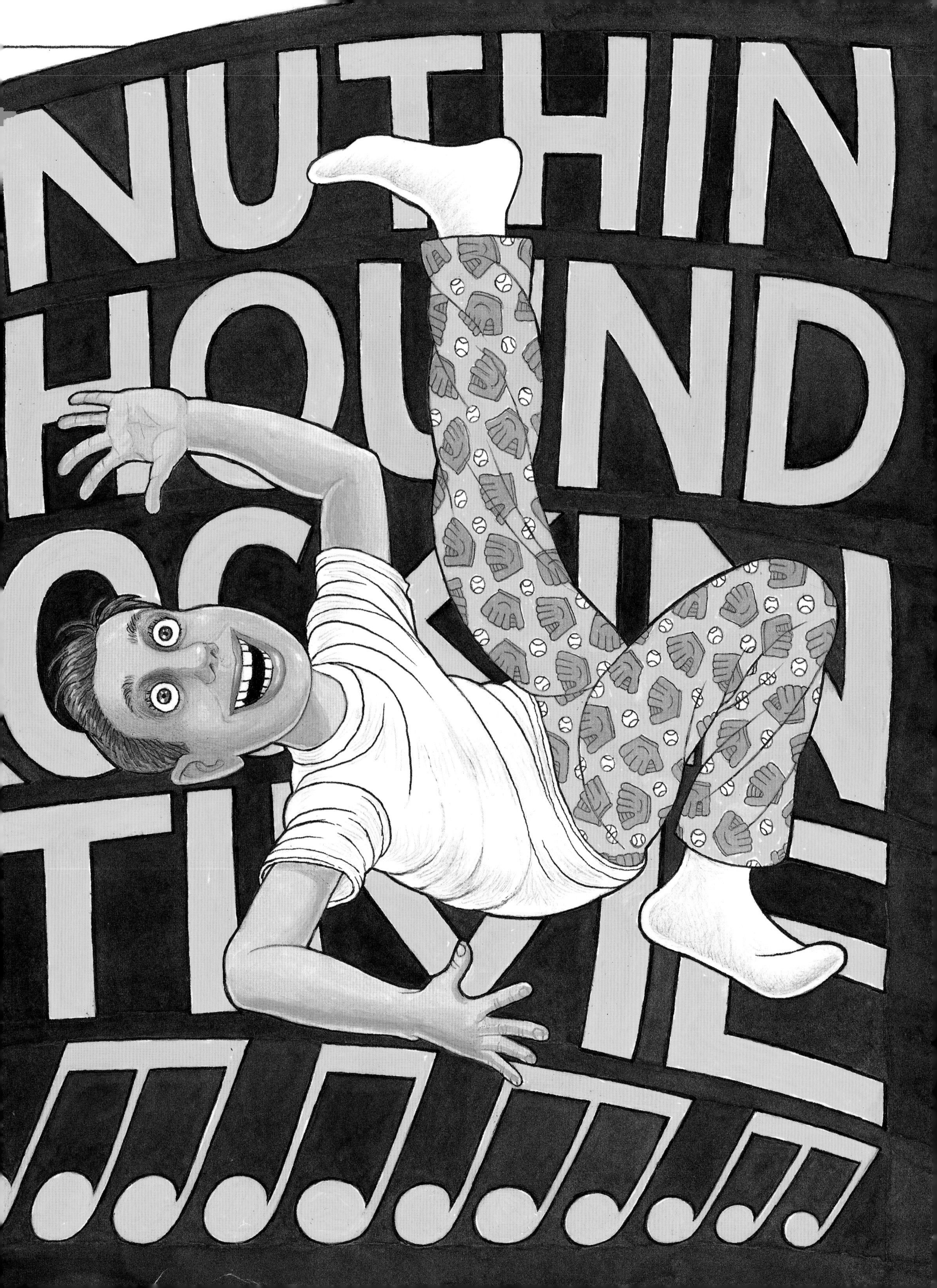
NUTHIN
HOUND

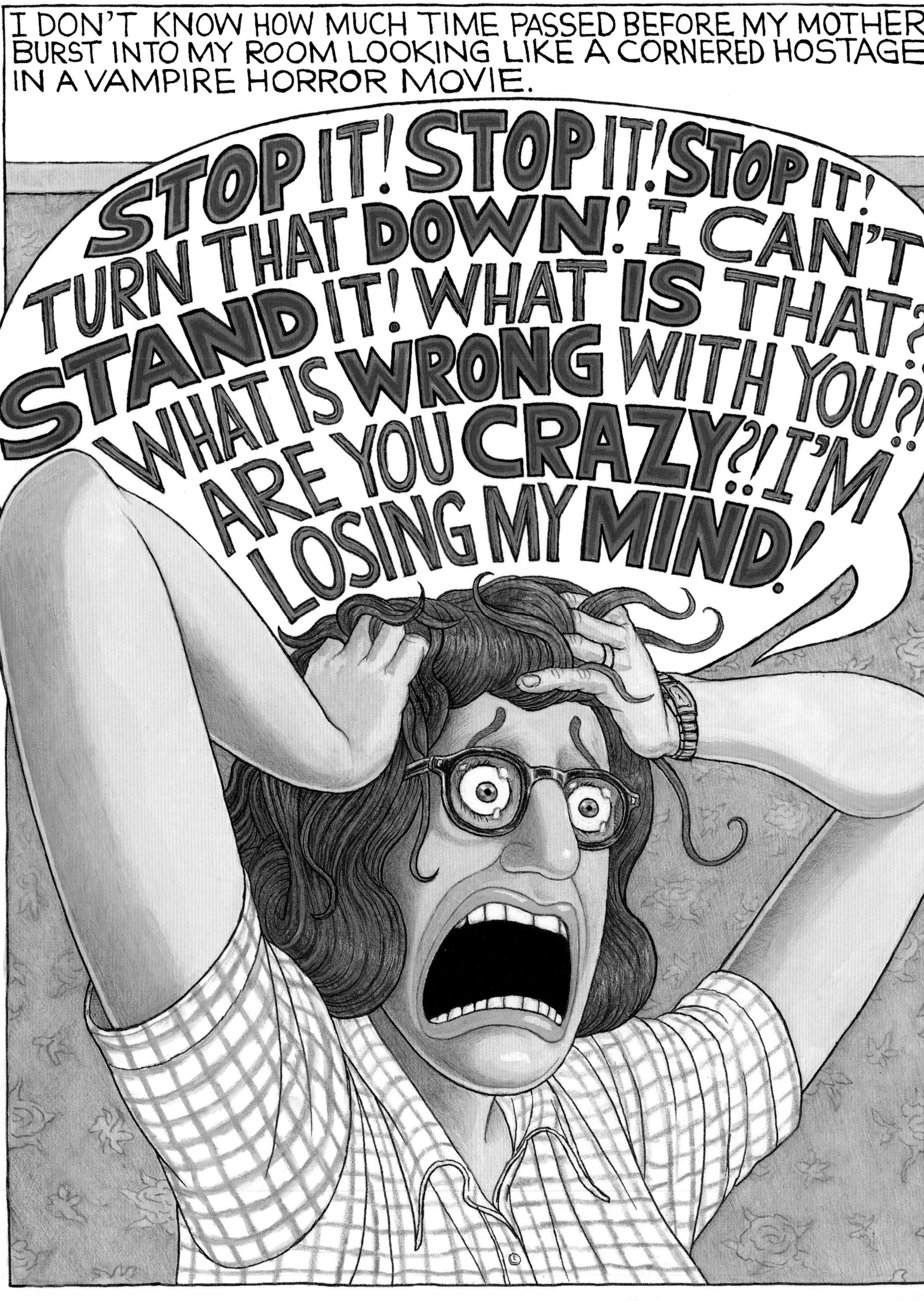
I DON'T KNOW HOW MUCH TIME PASSED BEFORE MY MOTHER BURST INTO MY ROOM LOOKING LIKE A CORNERED HOSTAGE IN A VAMPIRE HORROR MOVIE.
STOP IT! STOP IT! STOP IT! TURN THAT DOWN! I CAN'T STAND IT! WHAT IS THAT?! WHAT IS WRONG WITH YOU?! ARE YOU CRAZY?! I'M LOSING MY MIND!

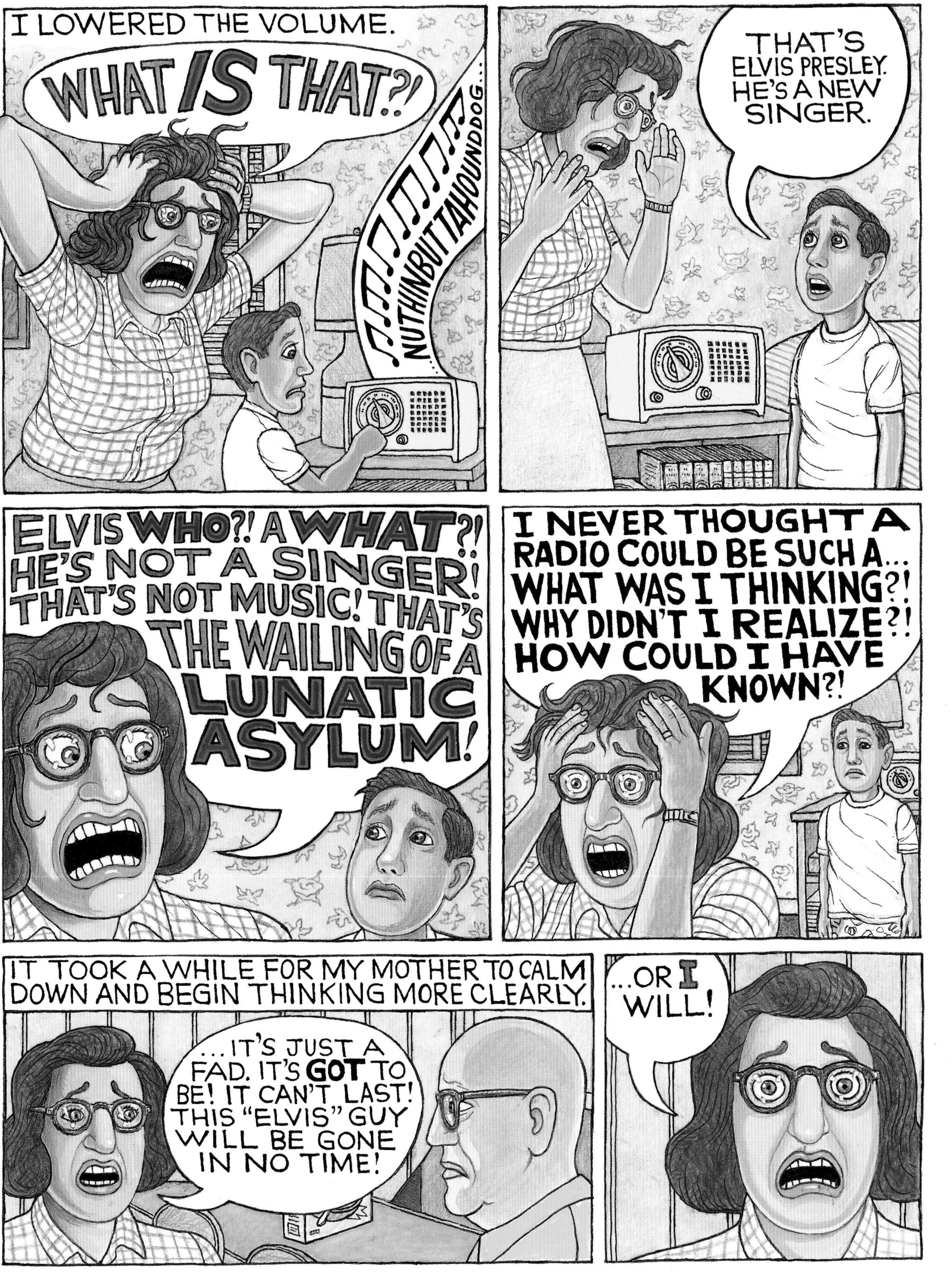
I LOWERED THE VOLUME.
WHAT IS THAT?!
NUTHINBUTTAHOUNDDOG...
THAT'S ELVIS PRESLEY. HE'S A NEW SINGER.
ELVIS WHO?! A WHAT?! HE'S NOT A SINGER! THAT'S NOT MUSIC! THAT'S THE WAILING OF A LUNATIC ASYLUM!
I NEVER THOUGHT A RADIO COULD BE SUCH A... WHAT WAS I THINKING?! WHY DIDN'T I REALIZE?! HOW COULD I HAVE KNOWN?!
IT TOOK A WHILE FOR MY MOTHER TO CALM DOWN AND BEGIN THINKING MORE CLEARLY.
...IT'S JUST A FAD. IT'S GOT TO BE! IT CAN'T LAST! THIS "ELVIS" GUY WILL BE GONE IN NO TIME!
...OR I WILL!

BUT ELVIS DID LAST. DAY TO DAY, MONTH TO MONTH, ELVIS KEPT GETTING BIGGER AND BIGGER AND BIGGER. AND THERE WAS POOR MOM, FACING OFF AGAINST MUSIC HISTORY. THERE'D BE NO STOPPING HIM. HE WAS CHANGING THE WHOLE WORLD!

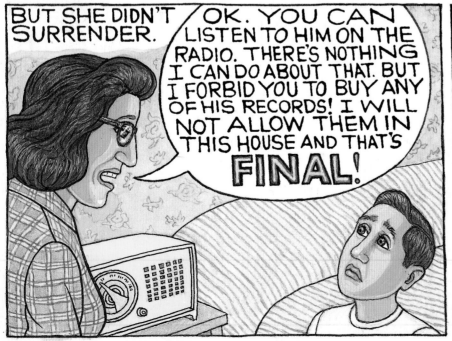

BUT SHE DIDN'T SURRENDER.

OK. YOU CAN LISTEN TO HIM ON THE RADIO. THERE'S NOTHING I CAN DO ABOUT THAT. BUT I FORBID YOU TO BUY ANY OF HIS RECORDS! I WILL NOT ALLOW THEM IN THIS HOUSE AND THAT'S FINAL!

AND IT WAS FINAL...

...FOR A WHILE.

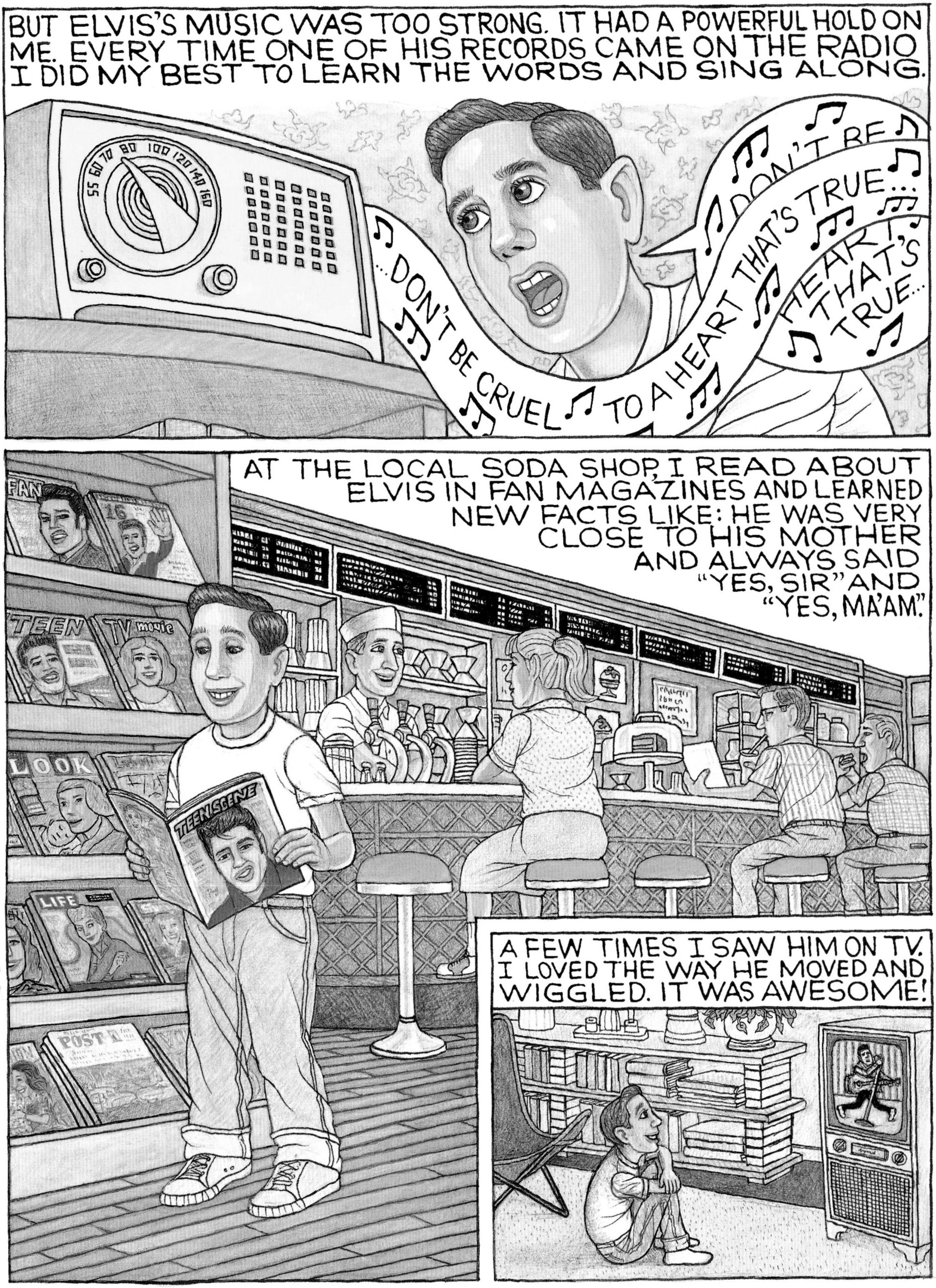
BUT ELVIS'S MUSIC WAS TOO STRONG. IT HAD A POWERFUL HOLD ON ME. EVERY TIME ONE OF HIS RECORDS CAME ON THE RADIO I DID MY BEST TO LEARN THE WORDS AND SING ALONG.
...DON'T BE CRUEL TO A HEART THAT'S TRUE...
DON'T BE
HEART THAT'S TRUE...
AT THE LOCAL SODA SHOP, I READ ABOUT ELVIS IN FAN MAGAZINES AND LEARNED NEW FACTS LIKE: HE WAS VERY CLOSE TO HIS MOTHER AND ALWAYS SAID "YES, SIR" AND "YES, MA'AM."
FAN
16
TEEN
TV movie
LOOK
LIFE
POST
TEEN SCENE
A FEW TIMES I SAW HIM ON TV. I LOVED THE WAY HE MOVED AND WIGGLED. IT WAS AWESOME!

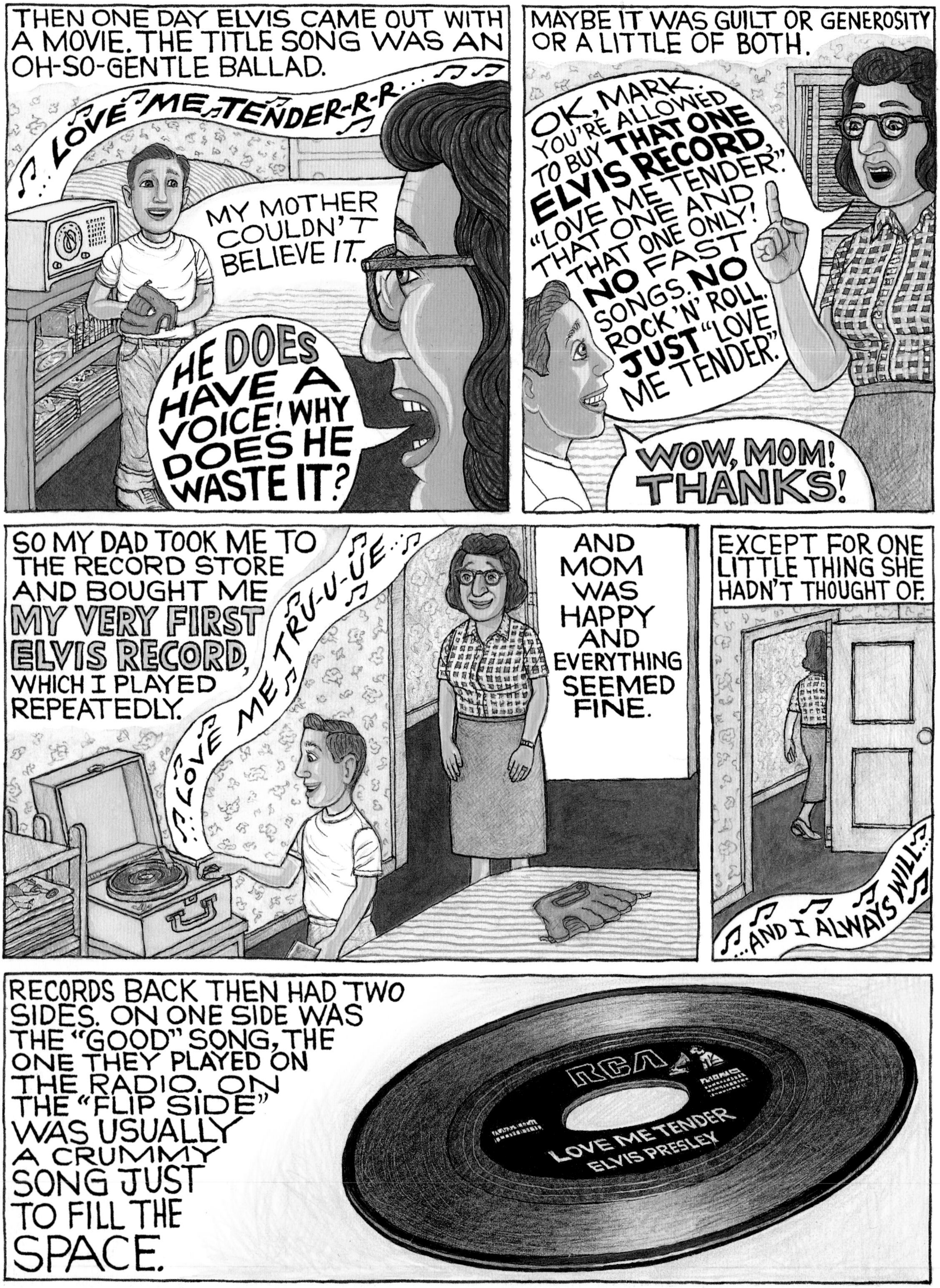
THEN ONE DAY ELVIS CAME OUT WITH A MOVIE. THE TITLE SONG WAS AN OH-SO-GENTLE BALLAD.
...LOVE ME TENDER-R-R...
MY MOTHER COULDN'T BELIEVE IT.
HE DOES HAVE A VOICE! WHY DOES HE WASTE IT?
MAYBE IT WAS GUILT OR GENEROSITY OR A LITTLE OF BOTH.
OK, MARK. YOU'RE ALLOWED TO BUY THAT ONE ELVIS RECORD, "LOVE ME TENDER." THAT ONE AND THAT ONE ONLY! NO FAST SONGS. NO ROCK 'N' ROLL. JUST "LOVE ME TENDER."
WOW, MOM! THANKS!
SO MY DAD TOOK ME TO THE RECORD STORE AND BOUGHT ME MY VERY FIRST ELVIS RECORD, WHICH I PLAYED REPEATEDLY.
...LOVE ME TRU-U-UE...
AND MOM WAS HAPPY AND EVERYTHING SEEMED FINE.
EXCEPT FOR ONE LITTLE THING SHE HADN'T THOUGHT OF.
...AND I ALWAYS WILL...
RECORDS BACK THEN HAD TWO SIDES. ON ONE SIDE WAS THE "GOOD" SONG, THE ONE THEY PLAYED ON THE RADIO. ON THE "FLIP SIDE" WAS USUALLY A CRUMMY SONG JUST TO FILL THE SPACE.
RCA
LOVE ME TENDER
ELVIS PRESLEY

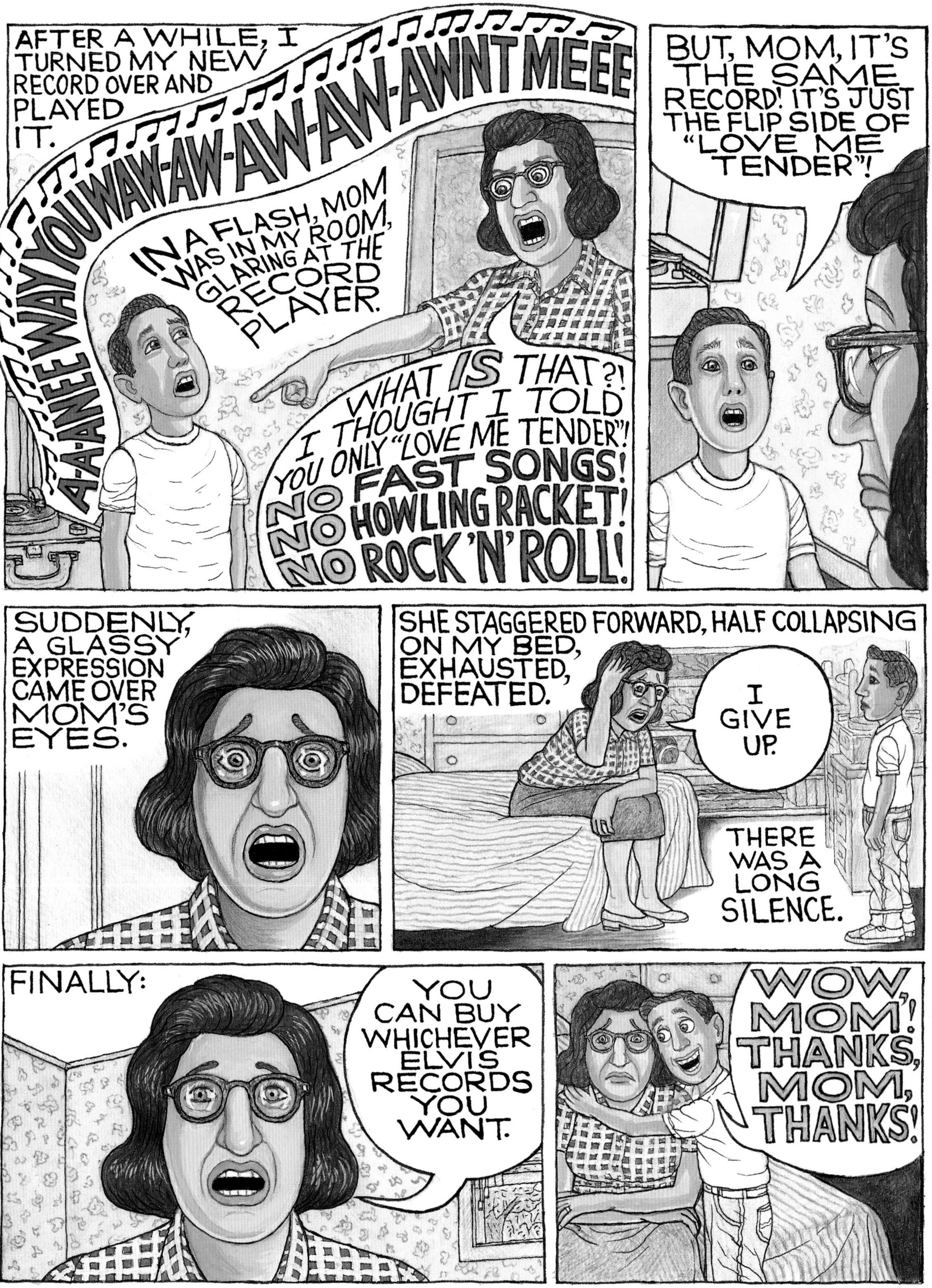
AFTER A WHILE, I TURNED MY NEW RECORD OVER AND PLAYED IT.
A-A-ANEE WAY YOU WAW-AW-AW-AW-AWNT MEEE
IN A FLASH, MOM WAS IN MY ROOM, GLARING AT THE RECORD PLAYER.
WHAT IS THAT?! I THOUGHT I TOLD YOU ONLY "LOVE ME TENDER"! NO FAST SONGS! NO HOWLING RACKET! NO ROCK 'N' ROLL!
BUT, MOM, IT'S THE SAME RECORD! IT'S JUST THE FLIP SIDE OF "LOVE ME TENDER"!
SUDDENLY, A GLASSY EXPRESSION CAME OVER MOM'S EYES.
SHE STAGGERED FORWARD, HALF COLLAPSING ON MY BED, EXHAUSTED, DEFEATED.
I GIVE UP.
THERE WAS A LONG SILENCE.
FINALLY:
YOU CAN BUY WHICHEVER ELVIS RECORDS YOU WANT.
WOW, MOM! THANKS, MOM, THANKS!

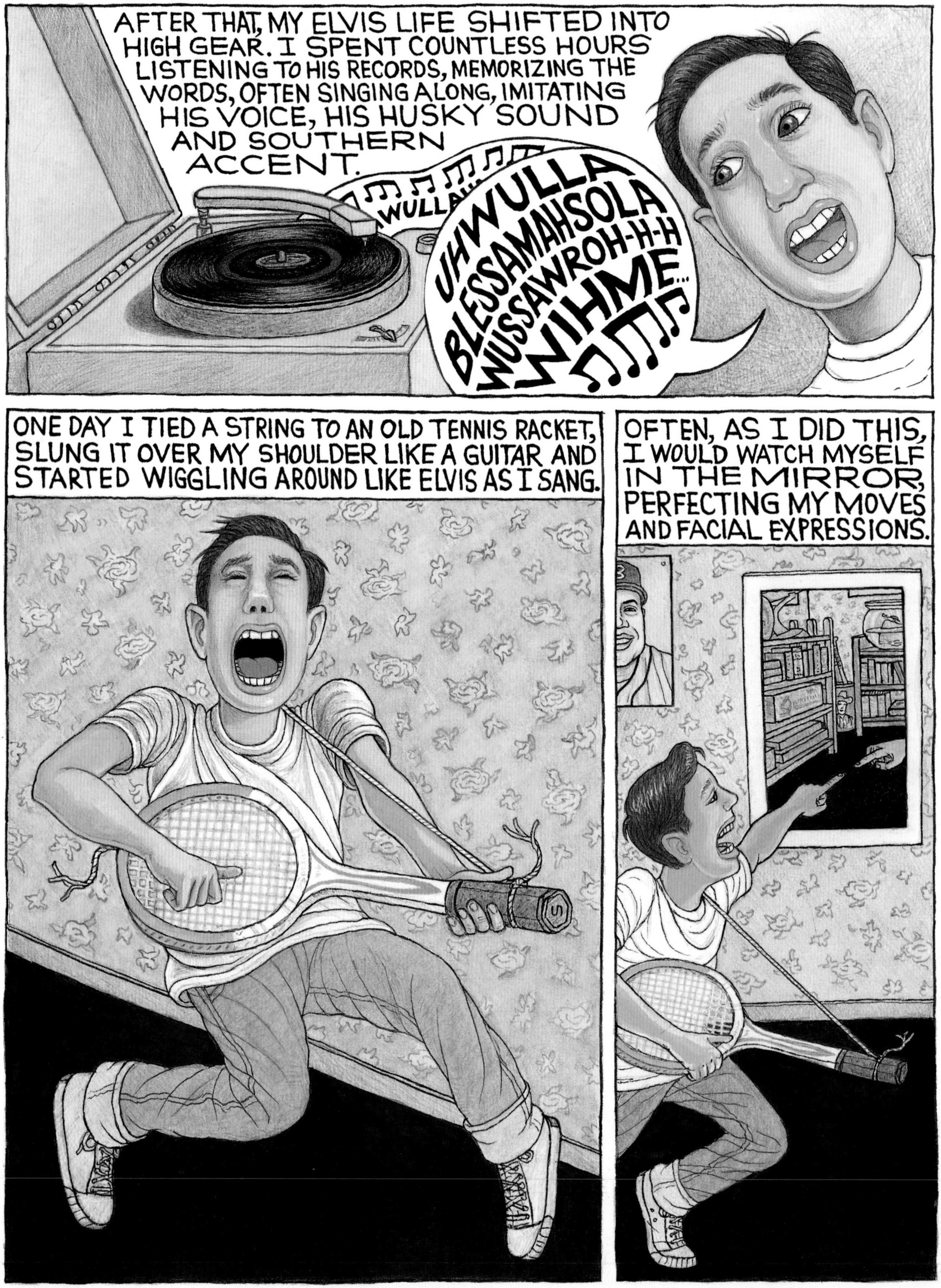
AFTER THAT, MY ELVIS LIFE SHIFTED INTO HIGH GEAR. I SPENT COUNTLESS HOURS LISTENING TO HIS RECORDS, MEMORIZING THE WORDS, OFTEN SINGING ALONG, IMITATING HIS VOICE, HIS HUSKY SOUND AND SOUTHERN ACCENT.
UHWULLA BLESSAMAHSOLA WUSSAWROH-H-H WIHME...
ONE DAY I TIED A STRING TO AN OLD TENNIS RACKET, SLUNG IT OVER MY SHOULDER LIKE A GUITAR AND STARTED WIGGLING AROUND LIKE ELVIS AS I SANG.
OFTEN, AS I DID THIS, I WOULD WATCH MYSELF IN THE MIRROR, PERFECTING MY MOVES AND FACIAL EXPRESSIONS.

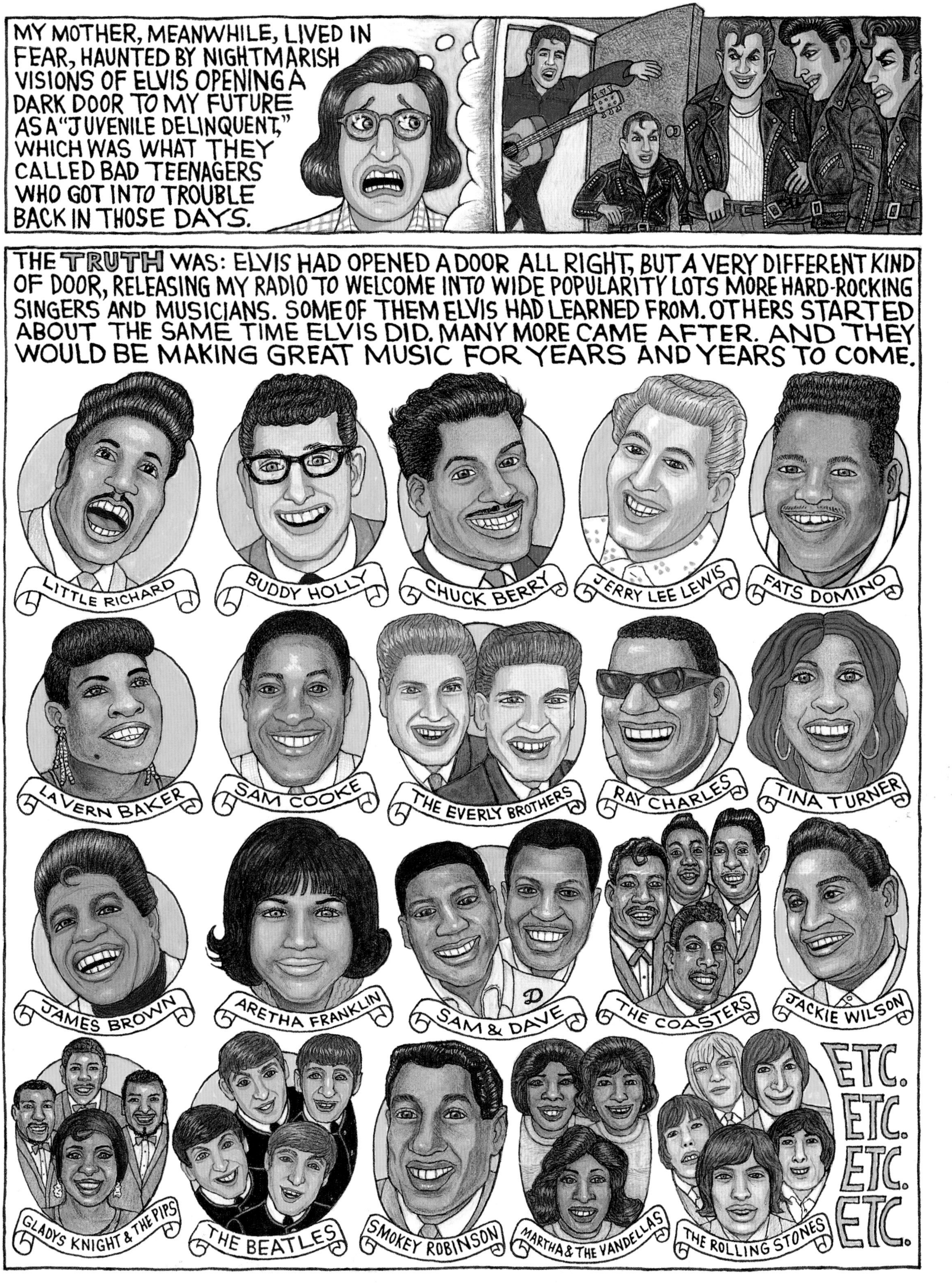
MY MOTHER, MEANWHILE, LIVED IN FEAR, HAUNTED BY NIGHTMARISH VISIONS OF ELVIS OPENING A DARK DOOR TO MY FUTURE AS A "JUVENILE DELINQUENT," WHICH WAS WHAT THEY CALLED BAD TEENAGERS WHO GOT INTO TROUBLE BACK IN THOSE DAYS.
THE TRUTH WAS: ELVIS HAD OPENED A DOOR ALL RIGHT, BUT A VERY DIFFERENT KIND OF DOOR, RELEASING MY RADIO TO WELCOME INTO WIDE POPULARITY LOTS MORE HARD-ROCKING SINGERS AND MUSICIANS. SOME OF THEM ELVIS HAD LEARNED FROM. OTHERS STARTED ABOUT THE SAME TIME ELVIS DID. MANY MORE CAME AFTER. AND THEY WOULD BE MAKING GREAT MUSIC FOR YEARS AND YEARS TO COME.
LITTLE RICHARD
BUDDY HOLLY
CHUCK BERRY
JERRY LEE LEWIS
FATS DOMINO
LAVERN BAKER
SAM COOKE
THE EVERLY BROTHERS
RAY CHARLES
TINA TURNER
JAMES BROWN
ARETHA FRANKLIN
SAM & DAVE
THE COASTERS
JACKIE WILSON
GLADYS KNIGHT & THE PIPS
THE BEATLES
SMOKEY ROBINSON
MARTHA & THE VANDELLAS
THE ROLLING STONES
ETC. ETC. ETC. ETC.

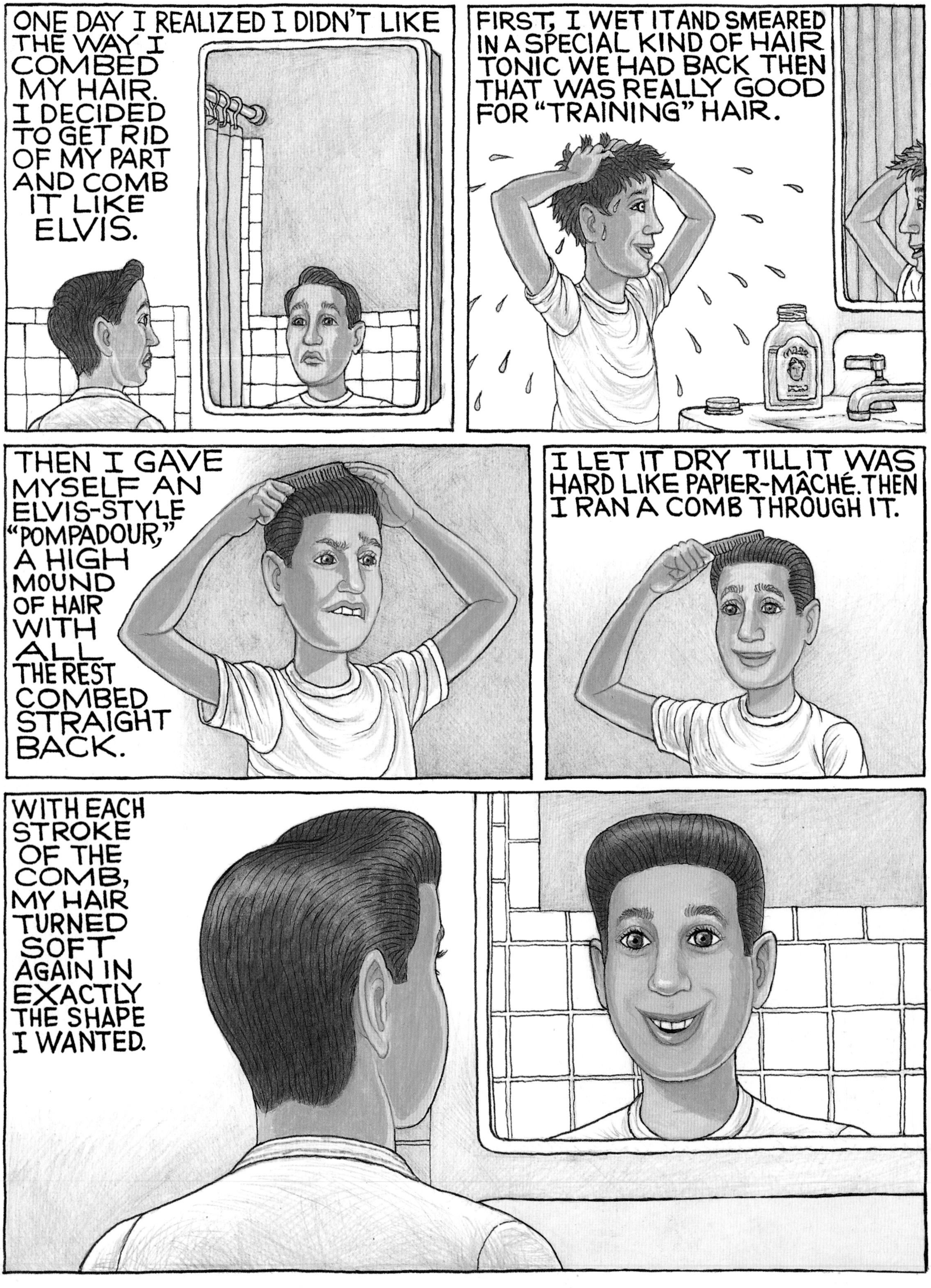
ONE DAY I REALIZED I DIDN'T LIKE THE WAY I COMBED MY HAIR. I DECIDED TO GET RID OF MY PART AND COMB IT LIKE ELVIS.
FIRST, I WET IT AND SMEARED IN A SPECIAL KIND OF HAIR TONIC WE HAD BACK THEN THAT WAS REALLY GOOD FOR "TRAINING" HAIR.
THEN I GAVE MYSELF AN ELVIS-STYLE "POMPADOUR," A HIGH MOUND OF HAIR WITH ALL THE REST COMBED STRAIGHT BACK.
I LET IT DRY TILL IT WAS HARD LIKE PAPIER-MÂCHÉ. THEN I RAN A COMB THROUGH IT.
WITH EACH STROKE OF THE COMB, MY HAIR TURNED SOFT AGAIN IN EXACTLY THE SHAPE I WANTED.

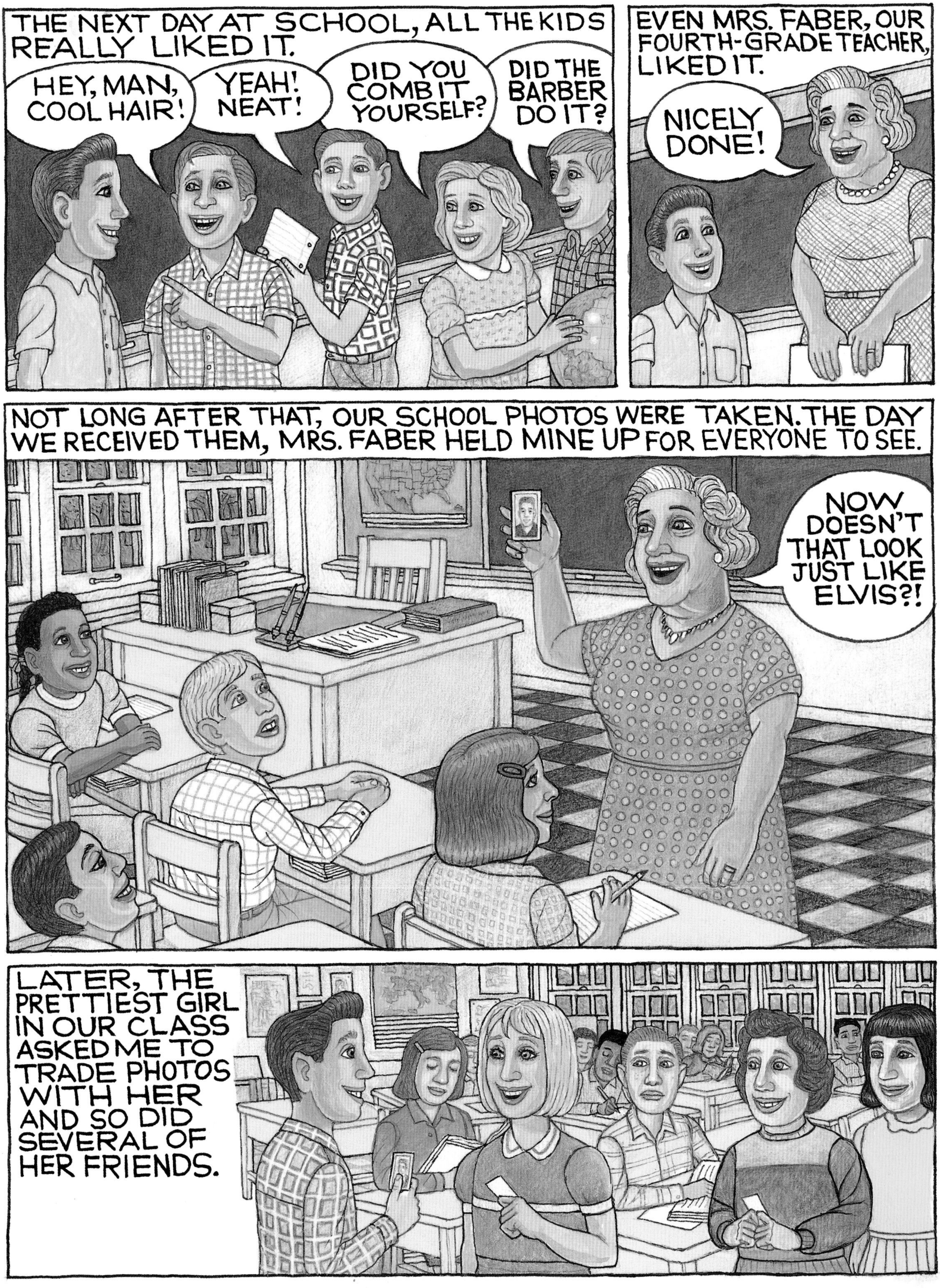
THE NEXT DAY AT SCHOOL, ALL THE KIDS REALLY LIKED IT.
HEY, MAN, COOL HAIR!
YEAH! NEAT!
DID YOU COMB IT YOURSELF?
DID THE BARBER DO IT?
EVEN MRS. FABER, OUR FOURTH-GRADE TEACHER, LIKED IT.
NICELY DONE!
NOT LONG AFTER THAT, OUR SCHOOL PHOTOS WERE TAKEN. THE DAY WE RECEIVED THEM, MRS. FABER HELD MINE UP FOR EVERYONE TO SEE.
NOW DOESN'T THAT LOOK JUST LIKE ELVIS?!
LATER, THE PRETTIEST GIRL IN OUR CLASS ASKED ME TO TRADE PHOTOS WITH HER AND SO DID SEVERAL OF HER FRIENDS.

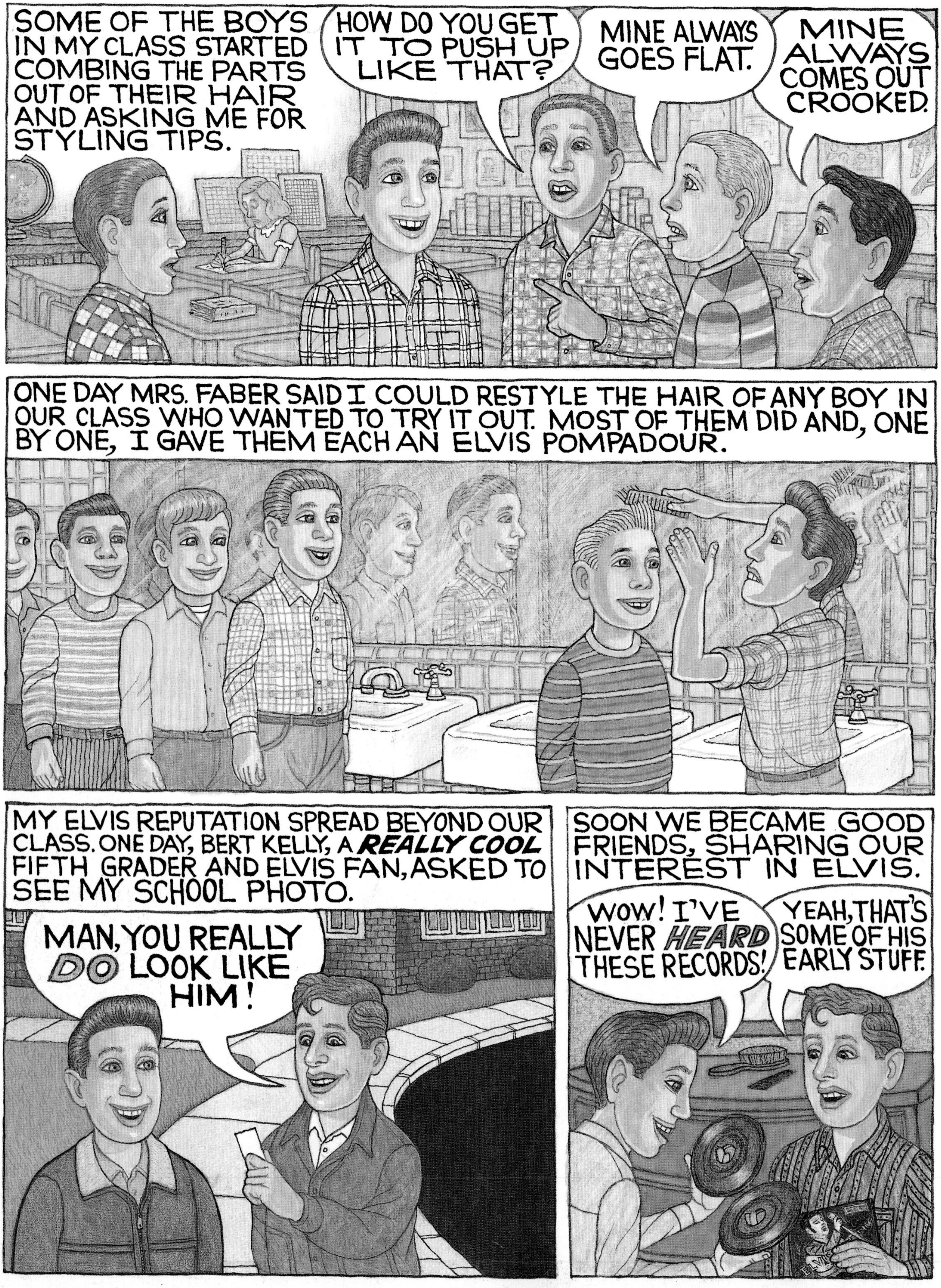
SOME OF THE BOYS IN MY CLASS STARTED COMBING THE PARTS OUT OF THEIR HAIR AND ASKING ME FOR STYLING TIPS.
HOW DO YOU GET IT TO PUSH UP LIKE THAT?
MINE ALWAYS GOES FLAT.
MINE ALWAYS COMES OUT CROOKED.
ONE DAY MRS. FABER SAID I COULD RESTYLE THE HAIR OF ANY BOY IN OUR CLASS WHO WANTED TO TRY IT OUT. MOST OF THEM DID AND, ONE BY ONE, I GAVE THEM EACH AN ELVIS POMPADOUR.
MY ELVIS REPUTATION SPREAD BEYOND OUR CLASS. ONE DAY, BERT KELLY, A ***REALLY COOL*** FIFTH GRADER AND ELVIS FAN, ASKED TO SEE MY SCHOOL PHOTO.
MAN, YOU REALLY *DO* LOOK LIKE HIM!
SOON WE BECAME GOOD FRIENDS, SHARING OUR INTEREST IN ELVIS.
WOW! I'VE NEVER *HEARD* THESE RECORDS!
YEAH, THAT'S SOME OF HIS EARLY STUFF.

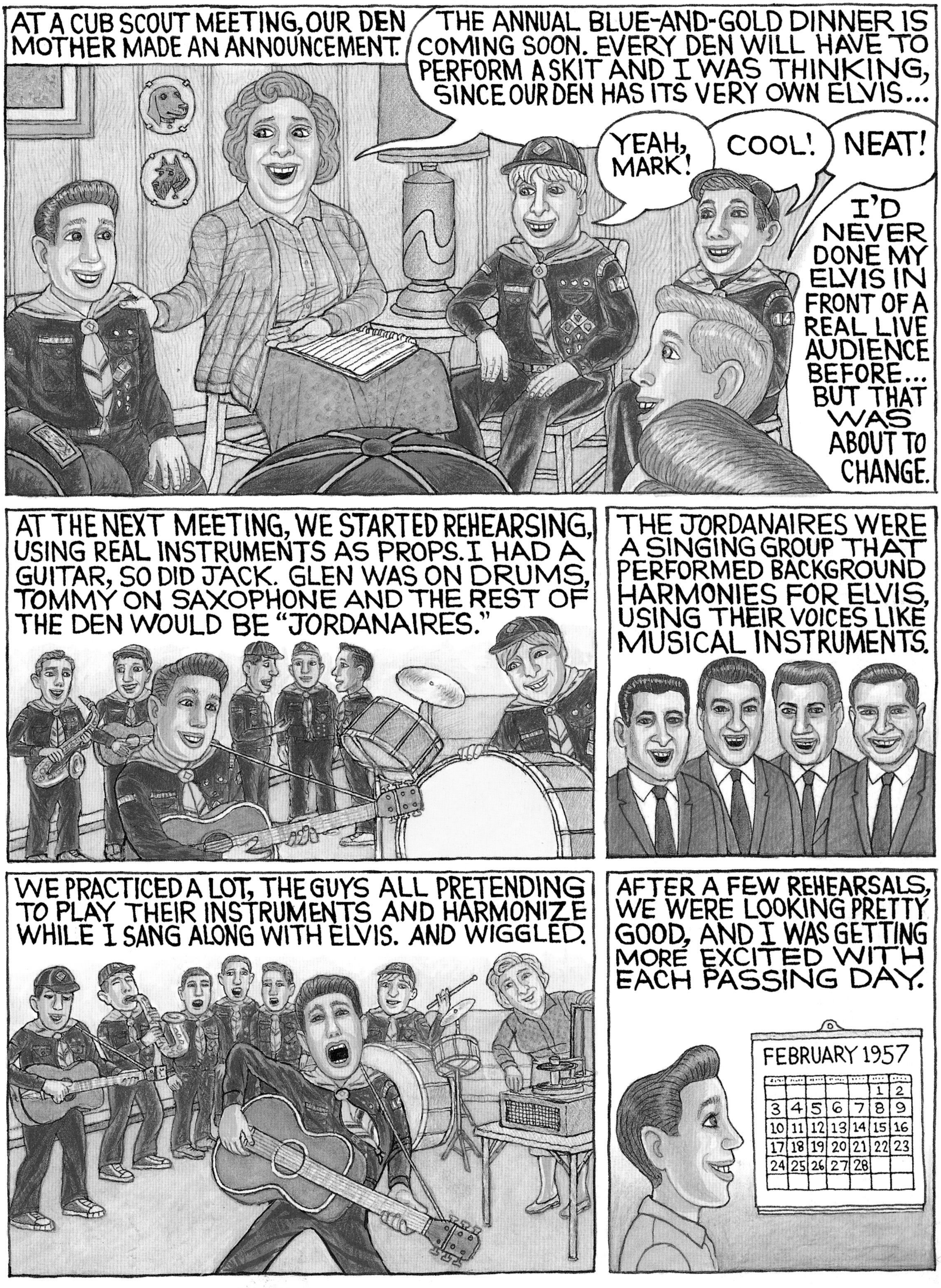
AT A CUB SCOUT MEETING, OUR DEN MOTHER MADE AN ANNOUNCEMENT.
THE ANNUAL BLUE-AND-GOLD DINNER IS COMING SOON. EVERY DEN WILL HAVE TO PERFORM A SKIT AND I WAS THINKING, SINCE OUR DEN HAS ITS VERY OWN ELVIS...
YEAH, MARK!
COOL!
NEAT!
I'D NEVER DONE MY ELVIS IN FRONT OF A REAL LIVE AUDIENCE BEFORE... BUT THAT WAS ABOUT TO CHANGE.
AT THE NEXT MEETING, WE STARTED REHEARSING, USING REAL INSTRUMENTS AS PROPS. I HAD A GUITAR, SO DID JACK. GLEN WAS ON DRUMS, TOMMY ON SAXOPHONE AND THE REST OF THE DEN WOULD BE "JORDANAIRES."
THE JORDANAIRES WERE A SINGING GROUP THAT PERFORMED BACKGROUND HARMONIES FOR ELVIS, USING THEIR VOICES LIKE MUSICAL INSTRUMENTS.
WE PRACTICED A LOT, THE GUYS ALL PRETENDING TO PLAY THEIR INSTRUMENTS AND HARMONIZE WHILE I SANG ALONG WITH ELVIS. AND WIGGLED.
AFTER A FEW REHEARSALS, WE WERE LOOKING PRETTY GOOD, AND I WAS GETTING MORE EXCITED WITH EACH PASSING DAY.
FEBRUARY 1957
1 2
3 4 5 6 7 8 9
10 11 12 13 14 15 16
17 18 19 20 21 22 23
24 25 26 27 28

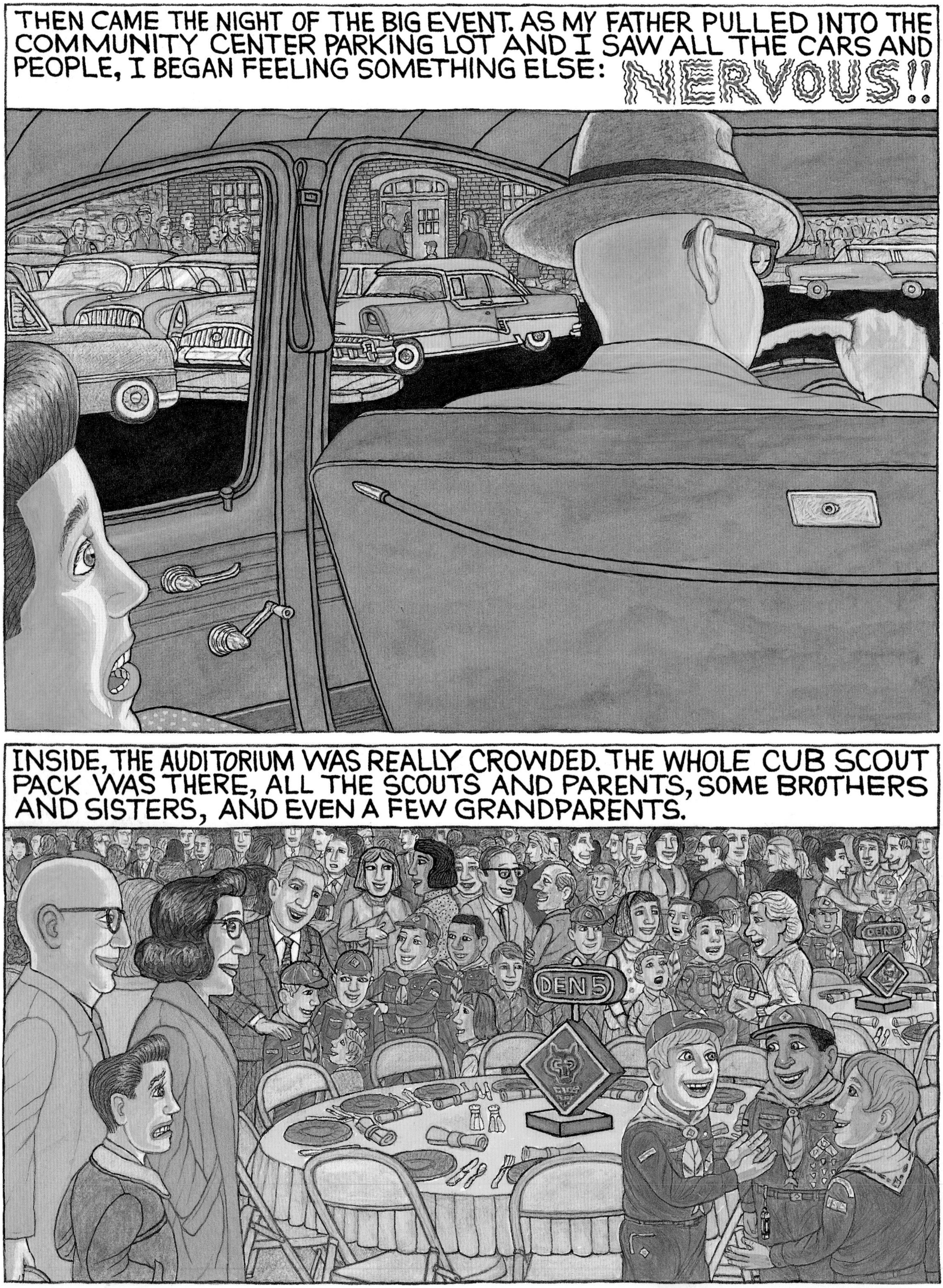
THEN CAME THE NIGHT OF THE BIG EVENT. AS MY FATHER PULLED INTO THE COMMUNITY CENTER PARKING LOT AND I SAW ALL THE CARS AND PEOPLE, I BEGAN FEELING SOMETHING ELSE: NERVOUS!!
INSIDE, THE AUDITORIUM WAS REALLY CROWDED. THE WHOLE CUB SCOUT PACK WAS THERE, ALL THE SCOUTS AND PARENTS, SOME BROTHERS AND SISTERS, AND EVEN A FEW GRANDPARENTS.
DEN 5

THE DINNER PART WENT BY IN A BLUR. THEN THE SKITS BEGAN. ONE BY ONE, EACH DEN APPEARED ONSTAGE. SOME OF THE SKITS WERE REALLY GOOD.

OUR DEN WAS SCHEDULED TO GO ON LAST. THE MORE I WAITED, THE MORE NERVOUS I GOT.

FINALLY, IT WAS TIME FOR US TO GO BACKSTAGE AND GET READY. I CHANGED INTO A JAZZY-LOOKING SHIRT I'D PICKED OUT FOR THE SHOW.

WITH AN EYEBROW PENCIL, I DREW MYSELF ELVIS-STYLE SIDEBURNS.

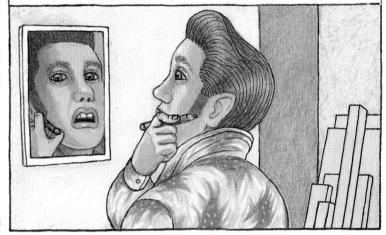

WE TOOK OUR PLACES ONSTAGE BEHIND THE CURTAIN. MY WHOLE BODY WAS SHAKING WITH NERVES.

LADIES AND GENTLEMEN, STRAIGHT FROM MEMPHIS, OUR SPECIAL SURPRISE GUEST: *ELVIS PRESLEY!*

THE CURTAIN OPENED. I SAW THE CROWD. ALL EYES ON ME! COULD THEY SEE HOW NERVOUS I WAS? COULD THEY TELL I WAS SHAKING?

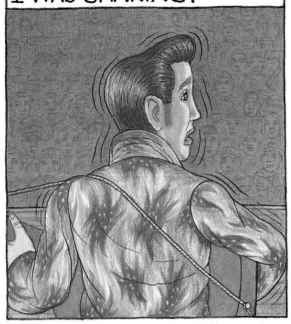

THE MUSIC BEGAN - LOUD AND CLEAR - AND ANOTHER FEELING SHOT THROUGH ME. THAT ELVIS FEELING! IT GOT ME MOVING AND SINGING.

SUDDENLY, I WASN'T SO NERVOUS. MY BODY WAS STILL SHAKING, BUT THAT ONLY MADE ME BETTER. SHAKING WAS WHAT ELVIS DID! AND, *BOY*, WAS I SHAKING! MOVING LIKE I'D NEVER MOVED BEFORE, DOING EVERY MOVE I'D PRACTICED ALL THOSE HOURS IN MY ROOM AND MAKING UP NEW ONES RIGHT THERE ON THE STAGE!

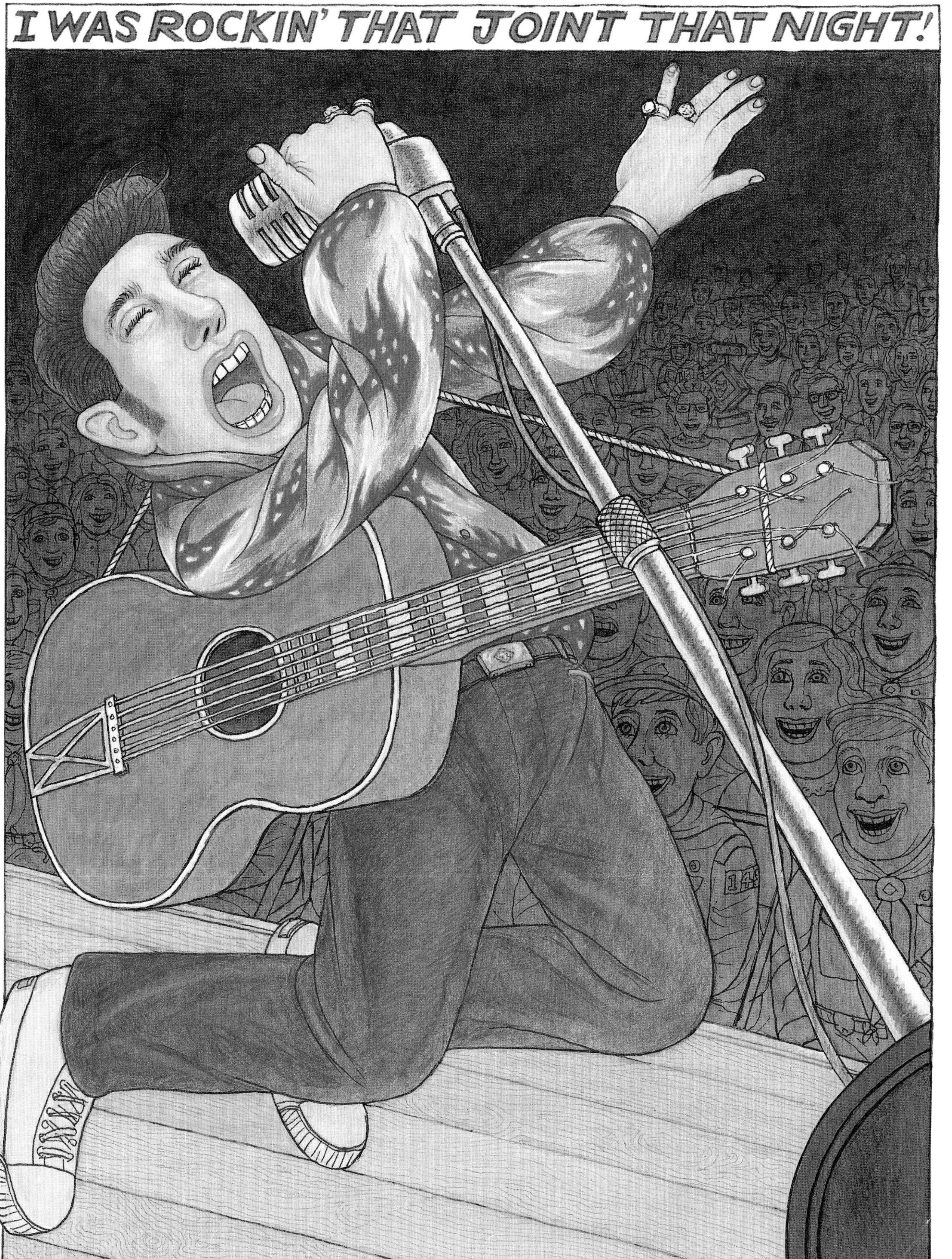
I WAS ROCKIN' THAT JOINT THAT NIGHT!

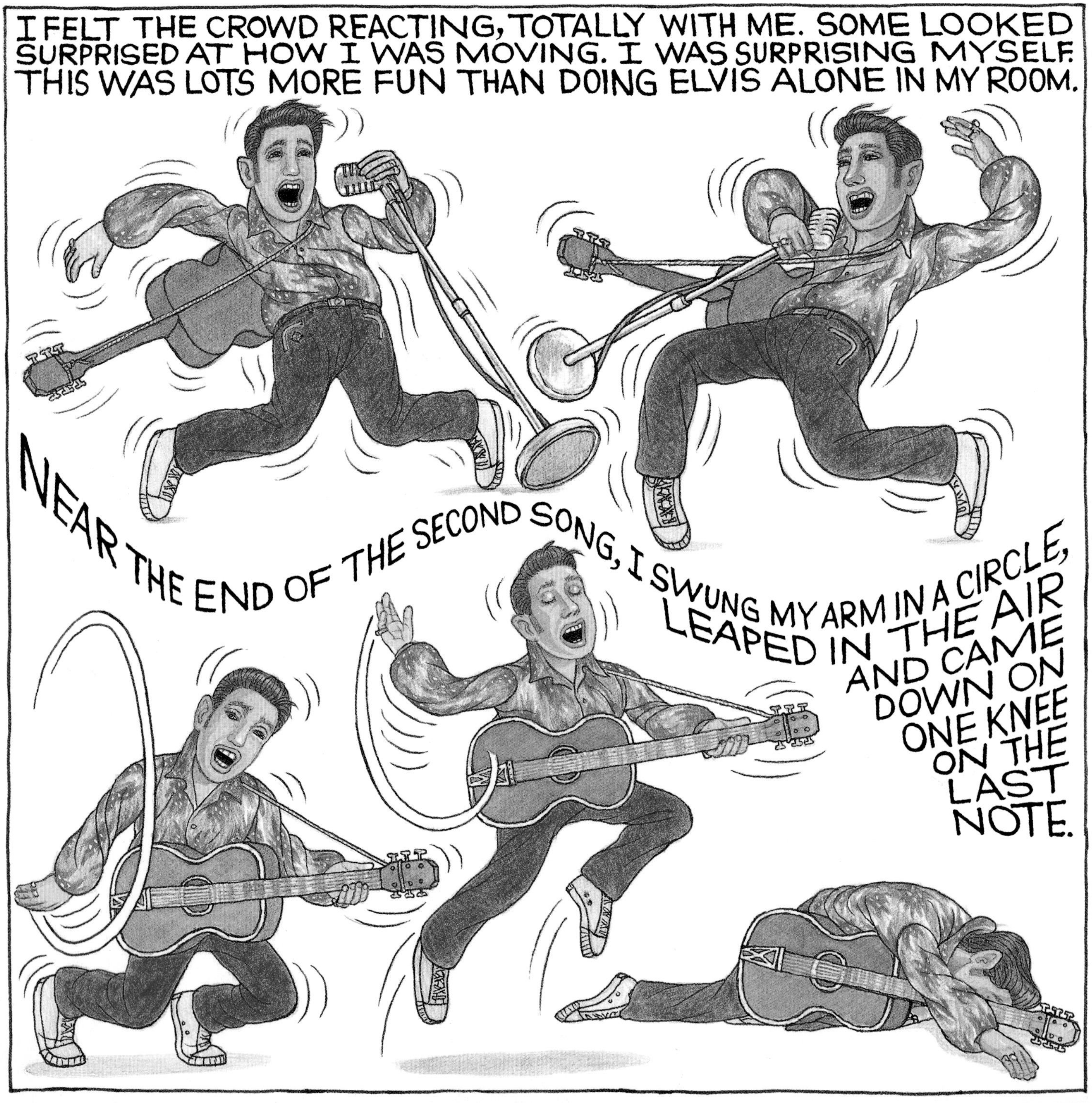
I FELT THE CROWD REACTING, TOTALLY WITH ME. SOME LOOKED SURPRISED AT HOW I WAS MOVING. I WAS SURPRISING MYSELF. THIS WAS LOTS MORE FUN THAN DOING ELVIS ALONE IN MY ROOM.
NEAR THE END OF THE SECOND SONG, I SWUNG MY ARM IN A CIRCLE, LEAPED IN THE AIR AND CAME DOWN ON ONE KNEE ON THE LAST NOTE.

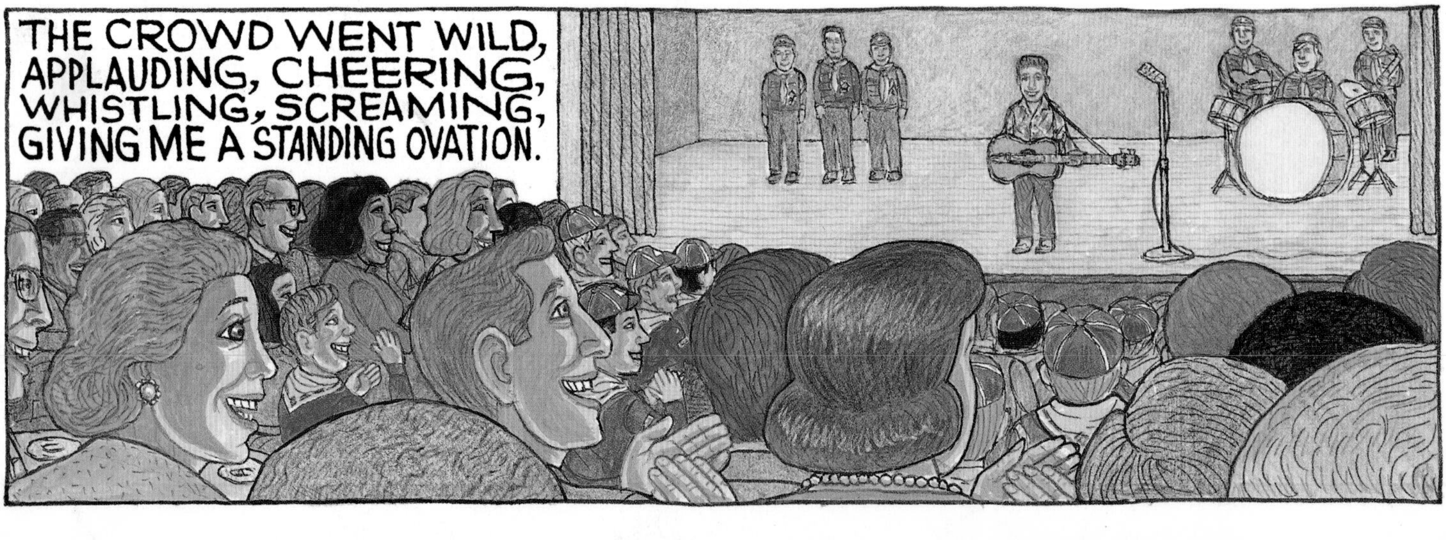
THE CROWD WENT WILD, APPLAUDING, CHEERING, WHISTLING, SCREAMING, GIVING ME A STANDING OVATION.

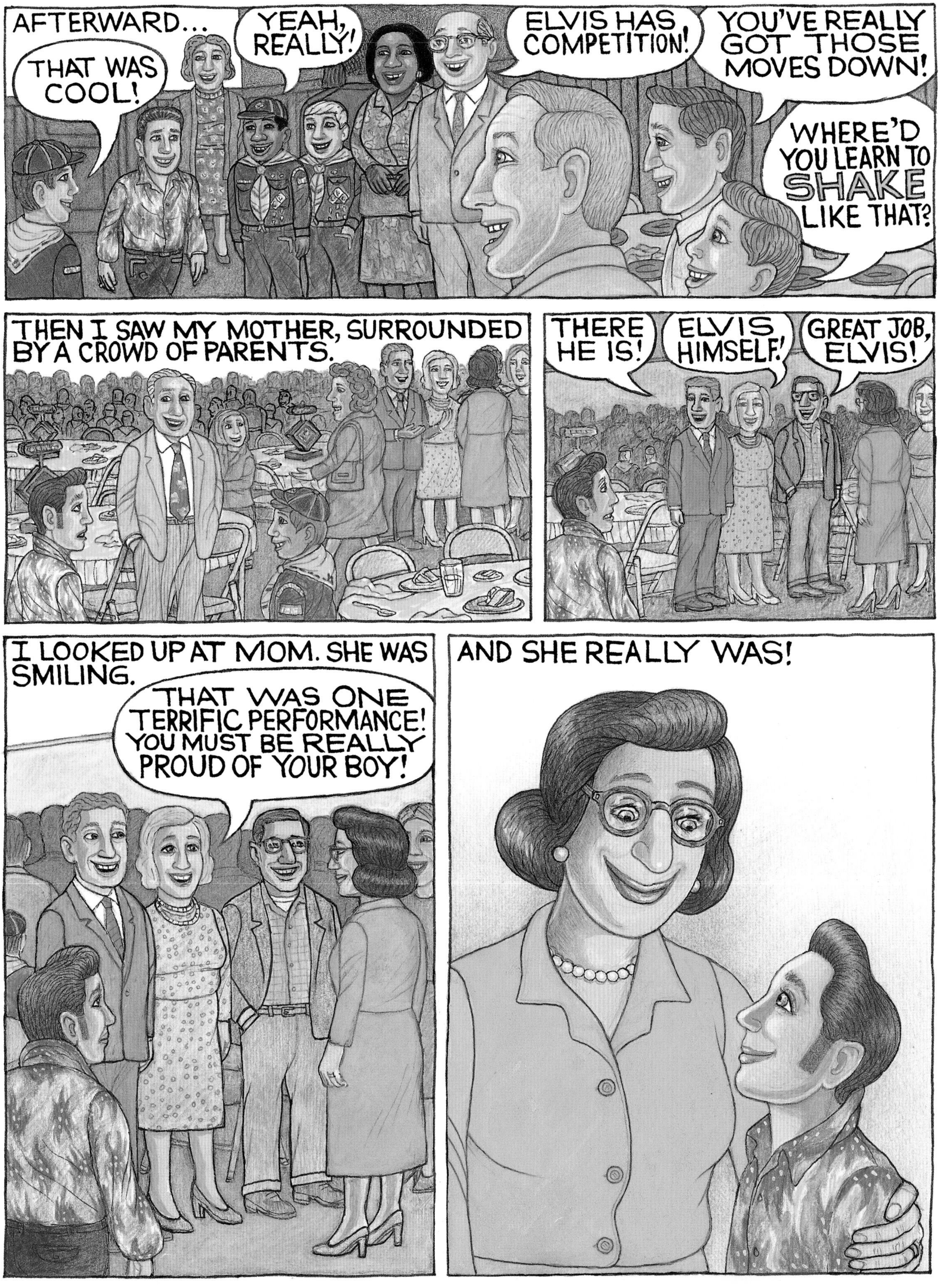
AFTERWARD...
THAT WAS COOL!
YEAH, REALLY!
ELVIS HAS COMPETITION!
YOU'VE REALLY GOT THOSE MOVES DOWN!
WHERE'D YOU LEARN TO SHAKE LIKE THAT?
THEN I SAW MY MOTHER, SURROUNDED BY A CROWD OF PARENTS.
THERE HE IS!
ELVIS HIMSELF!
GREAT JOB, ELVIS!
I LOOKED UP AT MOM. SHE WAS SMILING.
THAT WAS ONE TERRIFIC PERFORMANCE! YOU MUST BE REALLY PROUD OF YOUR BOY!
AND SHE REALLY WAS!

These are some photos of Elvis-related moments from my life:

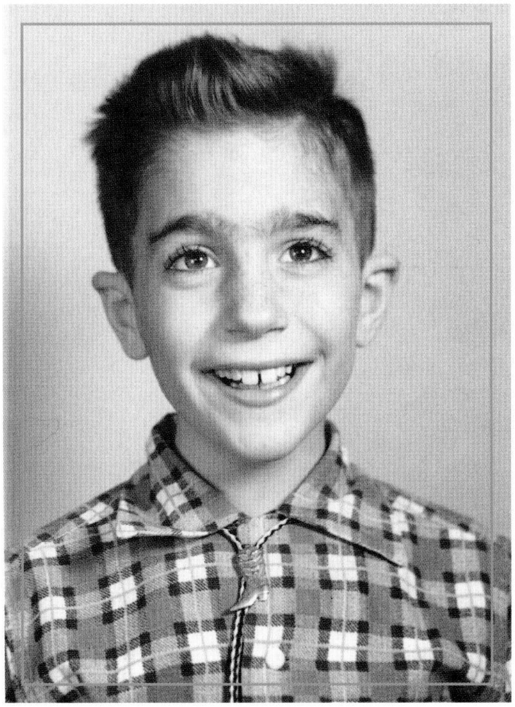

My third-grade school photo, the year I first discovered Elvis.

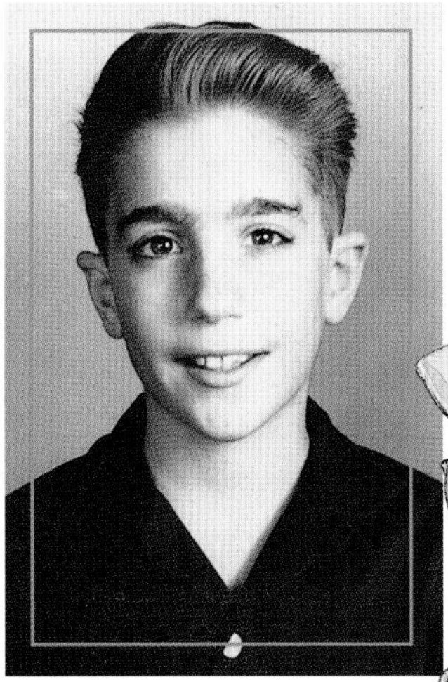

My fourth-grade school photo, which Mrs. Faber said looked like Elvis.

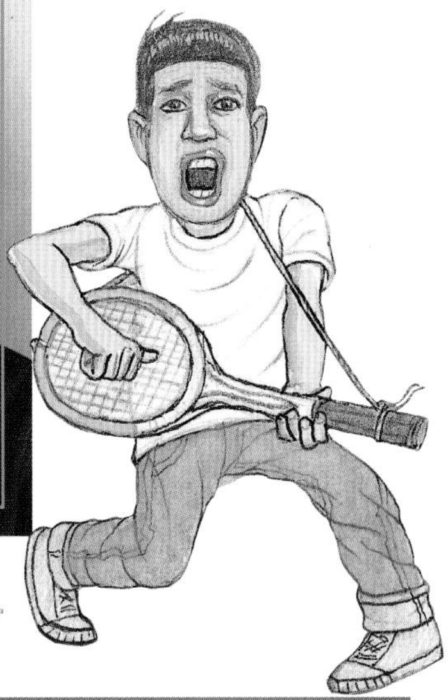

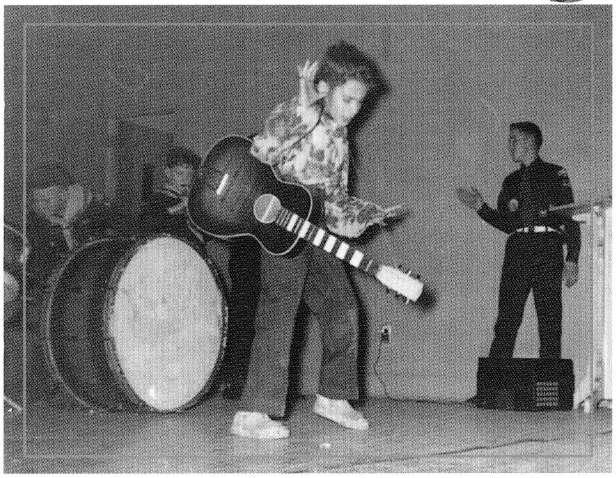

Me doing my Elvis at the Cub Scout dinner.

As I grew into adulthood in the years after the Cub Scout dinner, I often sang Elvis songs to myself, but rarely in front of other people. Then one night I went to a party at a friend's apartment. After a few hours, some people pulled out a couple of guitars, a microphone, and an amplifier that my friend owned and they started playing around with them.

I asked if they knew any Elvis songs. They did. So I took the mike and started singing and wiggling. Everyone loved it.

Then my friend got the idea that we should form a band and put on an Elvis show. Which we did. It was a big hit. Over the next several years, we put on a bunch of Elvis shows at private parties in various theaters, nightclubs, art schools, and lofts around Manhattan.

For many years, I was a political cartoonist for the *Washington Post.* In those days, the *Post* held a special dinner once a year for a small group of political cartoonists, journalists and politicians. At the end of each of those dinners, I would be called on to do my Elvis, a cappella.

In 1993, someone arranged for our group of cartoonists to have a one-hour visit with President Clinton and Vice President Gore in the Oval Office of the White House. The Vice President had once before seen me do my Elvis. He also knew that the President was an Elvis fan. After a while, he spoke up and said: “In his lifetime, Elvis only visited the White House once, but he’s here among us today.”

That was my cue to do my Elvis for the President. I took off my tie and jacket, turned up my collar, and did my rendition of “All Shook Up.”

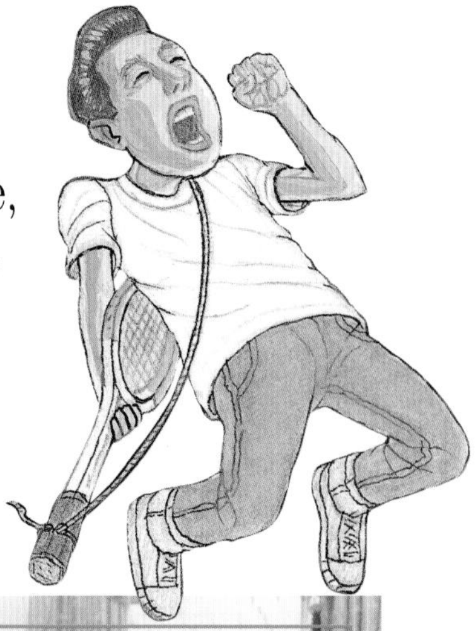

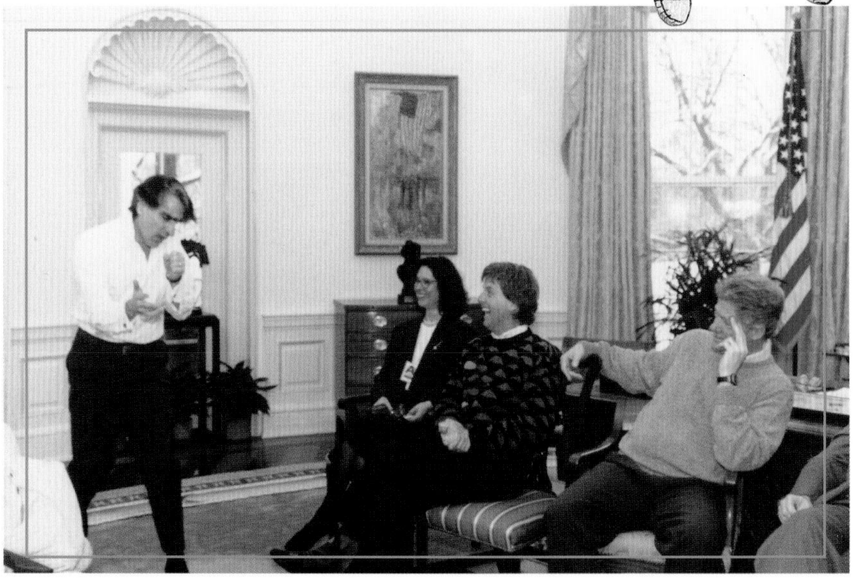

Official White House Photo

The President liked it so much he sent an aide upstairs to bring down an Elvis necktie he had in his closet, which he signed and gave to me.

I still have it (of course), safely tucked away, a valued memento and one of the many cool things that my love of Elvis has brought into my life.

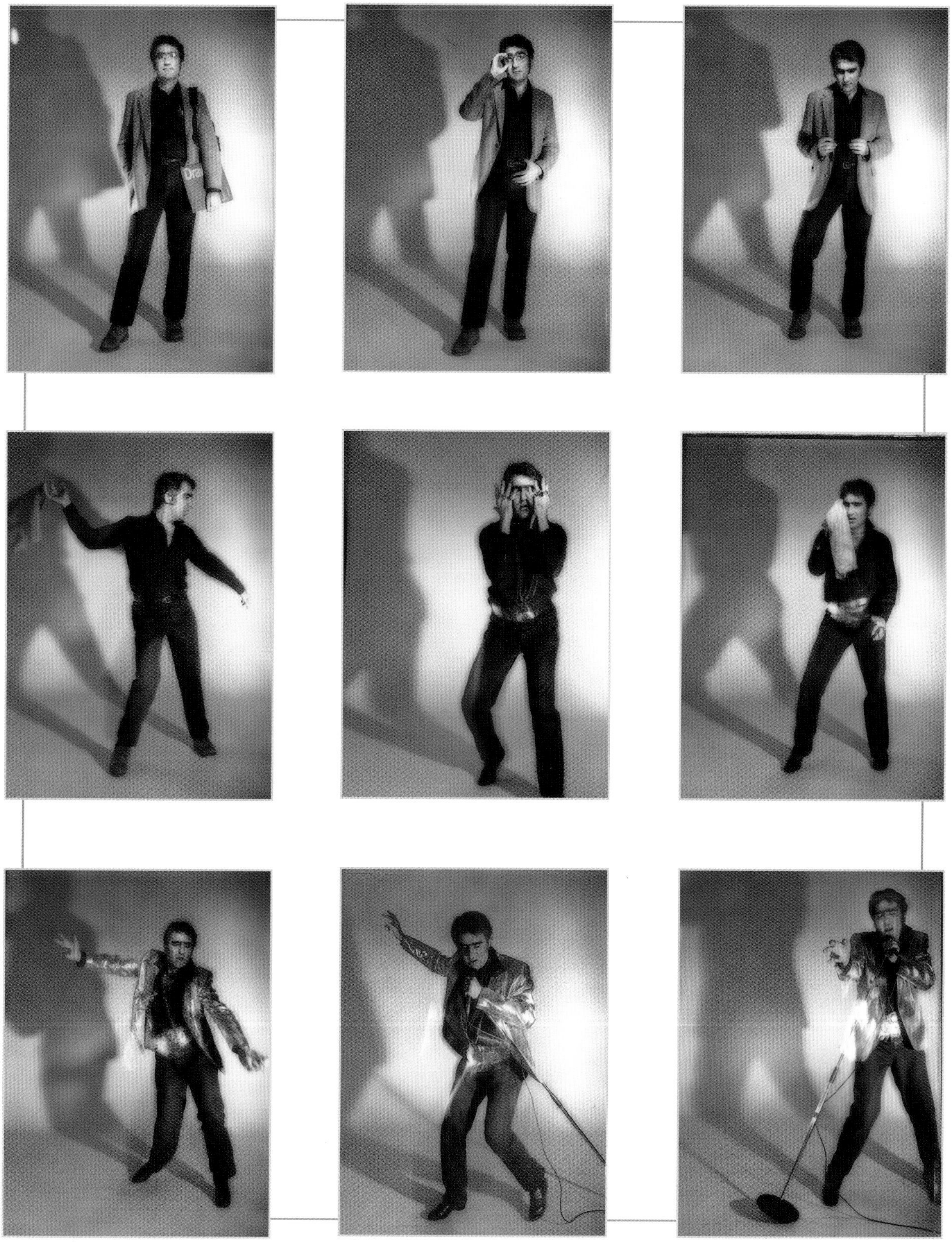

These photos show the transition from my real self into Elvis.

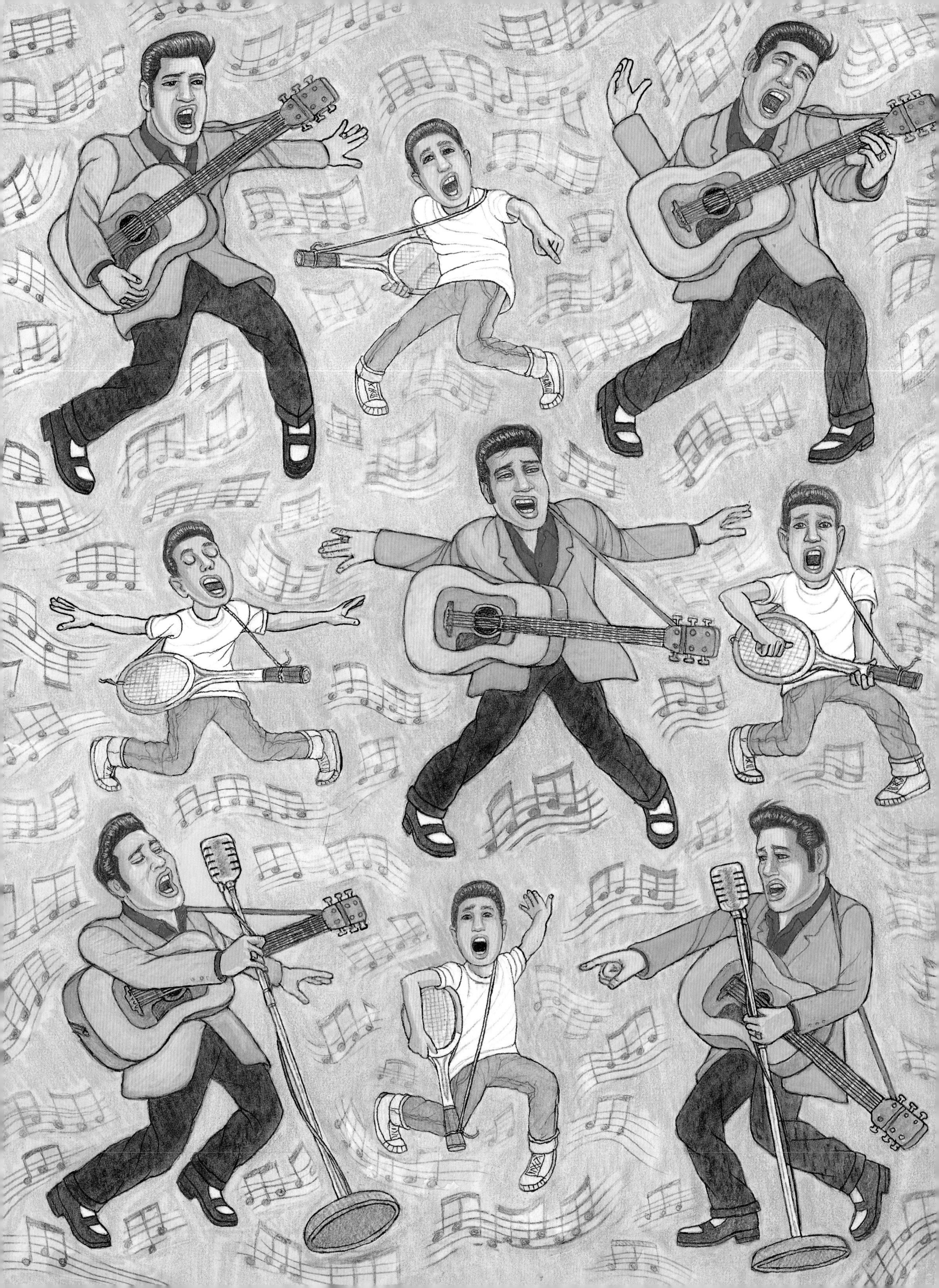